CLASSIC *f*M
Musical Anecdotes

Henry Kelly and John Foley

CLASSIC *f*M
Musical Anecdotes

FOREWORD BY
Lesley Garrett

Hodder & Stoughton

First published in Great Britain in 1998
by Hodder and Stoughton
A division of Hodder Headline PLC

British Library Cataloguing in Publication Data
A CIP catalogue record for this title is available
from the British Library.

ISBN 0 340 72881 7

Typeset by Palimpsest Book Production Limited,
Polmont, Stirlingshire
Printed and bound in Great Britain by
Mackays of Chatham PLC, Chatham Kent

Hodder and Stoughton
A division of Hodder Headline PLC
338 Euston Road
London NW1 3BH

CONTENTS

Henry Kelly, broadcaster, writer and television personality, broadcasts on the national independent radio station Classic FM on weekdays from 8am to noon. His programme is Classic FM's highest-rated programme, and in 1994 he was voted National Broadcaster of the Year in the prestigious Sony Awards. Following a rigorous Jesuit education at Belvedere College in his native Dublin, he read economics and English at University College, Dublin. He then joined *The Irish Times*, becoming Northern Editor based in Belfast during the early 1970s. His book *How Stormont Fell* is still essential reading for an understanding of those turbulent times. In 1976, he came to England to join the BBC Radio 4 current affairs programme *The World Tonight*. In 1981, he made his British television début as a presenter on the series *Game for a Laugh*. Numerous other television and radio programmes have since followed, including ten series of *Going for Gold* on BBC1.

He has always combined his broadcasting activities with writing, latterly for *The Times*, *Sporting Life*, and *The Spectator*. His most recent book was *Henry Kelly in the West of Ireland*, a historical archaeological, and slightly foodie guide to Ireland's Atlantic Coast.

John Foley is a writer, researcher, reference author, broadcaster and actor. As a writer, he has worked on a variety of commissions for the British Council, BBC (radio and television), Disney, Linguaphone, and Reader's Digest. He is the author of *The Guinness Encyclopedia of Signs & Symbols*, and co-author of *The Guinness Book of Beards and Moustaches*. Since 1987, he has been a regular contributor to the BBC World Service, where his writing includes language teaching programmes for BBC English, and features and numerous adaptations for 'Play of the Week' for World Service Drama. He also sets the monthly prize crossword for *Classic FM Magazine*, and currently runs the London office of *The School Times International*. As an actor, he has performed extensively throughout Britain and the United States in theatre and on radio.

'Without music, life would be a mistake.'
FRIEDRICH NIETZSCHE, *The Twilight of the Idols*

'Classic music is th'kind that we keep thinkin'll turn
into a tune.'
FRANK MCKINNEY ('KIN') HUBBARD,
Comments of Abe Martin and His Neighbors

'Here's to music, joy of joys:
One man's music, another man's noise.'
ANON

To music and the people who make it
HENRY KELLY & JOHN FOLEY

FOREWORD

M USIC IS NOT A PROFESSION, it is a passion, and musicians are passionate people. I'm not talking about 'artistic temperament', because I don't believe that such a thing exists. Musicians' personalities come in all shapes and sizes, but the one thing they absolutely do share is a kind of heightened sensitivity to their life and work. Music is the universal language of emotion. The grandest opera or the simplest song can touch our deepest feelings more profoundly than any other art form. And after all, emotions are a musician's stock in trade: love, hate, grief, jealousy, despair, joy – we meet them all every working day. Being cool, calm and detached may be a fine and healthy way to react to life, but it's not our way. If it was, the world would be a much duller place. I am sure this is why the world of music is such a fertile source of anecdotes. But why do so many of them have to involve fat sopranos? There is a popular stereotype of a female opera singer with the build and emotional range of a brick outhouse. It used to make me so angry that I finally had a T-shirt made for myself which proudly proclaimed, 'IT AIN'T OVER TILL THE THIN LADY ACTS'.

Henry and John have put together the most fabulous collection of stories that give a wonderful insight into the characters behind the music that you and I love so much. Some of them will make you smile, a lot of them will make you laugh, and some may even make you cry, but what else do you expect when you enter the world of masters of emotional manipulation? Read and enjoy!

LESLEY GARRETT

If music be . . .

THERE'S NO WAY of knowing when the first joke or story was made about music and who made it. It could be, of course, that the introduction of musical anecdotes, jokes, stories, interesting pieces of information and the like, all of which we hope you'll enjoy in these pages, occurs in every generation and always has. Just as myths have a habit of turning up in roughly similar guise in different traditions so, I suppose, tall tales, 'stop me if you've heard this one', stories and fun items probably have the same cyclical recurrence as the regularity with which we wait ages for a bus and three turn up at once.

There is apparently in some circles a debate as to who was the father of music. Italians like to offer Palestrina (1529–94) as the 'prince of musicians', while dipping the toe in mythology and the Bible we find the suggestion in Genesis that Jubal was 'the father of all such as handle the harp and organ'. We didn't make the last bit up. Every full-witted and even half-witted playwright, poet, novelist, and versifier has had a go at dragging music into their works, sometimes to support something which was worthy of the said support and at other times to try and draw attention away from rubbish. You know what we mean, and there's plenty of evidence around to support the case: bad television programmes trying to fool you into thinking they're good by having Mahler on the gramophone and rotten Hollywood epics which think we'll be fooled by the on-screen nonsense if there's a soppy string quartet in the background.

It's amazing the number of star members of the human race who couldn't hack music at all. Edmund Burke hated it all; Byron admitted he had no ear for it and once swore that neither vocal nor instrumental music did anything for him; Dr Johnson, David Hume, Robert Peel, William Pitt, the Irish Liberator, Daniel O'Connell, and Alexander Pope all had serious reservations about what we love and cherish today as the world's most beautiful music. Pope even said that if he had to listen to music, he preferred 'a street organ to a Handel oratorio'. One of the great ironies must be that Sir Walter Scott (one of whose novels gave Donizetti the inspiration for *Lucia di Lammermoor*) had no feel or feeling for any type of music whatever. Plato saves us all by his suggestion that every planet has a siren who 'carols a most sweet song'.

So what have we to offer? Well, everything from what we would loosely call 'jokes' (a notorious substitute for conversation but useful to keep a struggling one going sometimes), true stories about music and musicians, things that actually happened, things that might have happened, and things that probably didn't but should have; all this plus a quote or two, and even the odd non-hilarious note to add to our knowledge about instruments, composers or performers.

It's a huge field, and many of the items you'll read

you may have heard before in some shape or form. Some have been overheard, some written down, some sent to us since we let friends – particularly musician friends – know what we were about. Others have been collected from already published works and either quoted here in full or rewritten.

As well as enjoying the reading we've done in the compilation of our anecdotes, we've also had great fun listening to other people's conversations on the subject we love dearly. One of the remarkable things has been the generosity of those from whom we have sought help in a simple, friendly sort of way. They know who they are, and we are grateful to them all. Listing them would be embarrassing, and, besides, if they saw their names in a book they might suddenly decide they wanted to be paid. Please!

Don't panic if you think you've read anything in a different form before: you probably have. But we reckon if something was worth telling once then, like a good radio play or a television sitcom that made you laugh first time round, it's worth repeating.

We feel that perhaps the most famous and over-worked musical quotation comes from that nice Mr Shakespeare, who had one of his characters launch themselves into: 'If music be the food of love, play on . . .' and on . . . and on . . . Our view is that if music be the food of love, how come rabbits can't play the piano? You have been warned.

Tucked away at the back of this volume we've included brief biographies of characters who appear more than three times (see 'Who's who'), and some technical terms. This book has been a duet (technical term, see 'What's what'!) between myself and my colleague, John Foley. The introductions to each section are my fault however, and I'd like to take this opportunity to thank John for his hard work and patience over the last few years. It has been fun, yes, but hard work, most of which was done by John. I am really grateful. I'd be grateful, too, if any readers who have stories of their own tucked away would like to pass them on for future editions, since I refuse to believe that the supply of viola stories, conductor stories and reports of the bizarre happenings of orchestras, behaviour patterns of composers and social activities of musicians in general has dried up!

Name that tunesmith
COMPOSERS AND COMPOSING

L ET'S FACE IT: they did it all, they wrote it, without them no music, no performers, certainly no books telling stories about the eccentricities of ... well, composers. I dread to think of the number of rain forests that have been cut down to provide the paper upon which the millions of words have been spilled on the lives, loves and works of the great and not-so-great men and women who have handed down to future generations – and indeed still continue so to do – what we call the world's most beautiful music. Yet there remains the notion that they were all rather intellectual and a bit stuffy, their heads in the musical clouds, their tempers short and their lives a constant riot of nothing more exciting than their compositions. A proper reading of their lives, as this section will I hope amply demonstrate, shows a different picture, one which offers a view of some of the musical greats as being more human than even some of their greatest admirers would wish to let on.

Mozart was a real lad! His companion, the Irish tenor Michael Kelly, has stories to tell of drinking bouts which would make English footballers look like teetotallers, of escapes to billiard halls (these being the only places where the police would not venture even to collect Wolfgang's accumulated debts), and of sexual flirtations that can only have inspired the more hilarious parts which were to appear in some of the world's great operas.

Vivaldi was officially a priest but, well, not quite what he appeared; Delius, until he went blind, loved cricket and even after that tragedy (the blindness, not English cricket!) was a regular at matches where the play was described to him by, among others, his colleague Eric Fenby and the critic Neville Cardus. Almost every composer tells the story in one shape or another of the empty page and the first few lines. All their lives are riddled with anxiety, frustration, hope and misery, despair and jocularity, and, mercifully, great success – if not in their lifetimes, then at least for our ears. It is salutary to reflect as we listen to Beethoven that he went deaf, that Mozart was buried in a pauper's grave, that Vivaldi's 'greatest hits' are a comparatively modern phenomenon many of which were unearthed only in the 1950s and 1960s and that many, many composers whom today we consider 'great' never heard their works performed in their own lifetimes.

A list of some of the names with which we are today familiar could, if you like, sound like a who's who of the eccentric: Mussorgsky was not totally with it most of the time and had most of his great works 'helped' by friends; Debussy was a chain-smoking fun-lover, but terrible with his friends; Brahms was as rich as they come, yet hardly spent money at all and had as his preferred evening meal fish and chips; and Beethoven, whom we revere as a demi-God, was by all accounts the most untidy man with many of his manuscripts being sullied by the circles left by either his beer-mugs or his chamber pots. A great crew all in all, composers, but wait until you read some of the things said about them!

&

'Before I compose a piece, I walk around it several times, accompanied by myself.'

ERIK SATIE; quoted in *Bulletin des Éditions Musicales*, Paris (December 1913)

When first performed by the Vienna Men's Choral Society in 1867, Johann Strauss II's *An der schönen blauen Donau*, better known as 'The Blue Danube', was less than favourably received. This was mainly because of some dreadful lyrics with 'political overtones' – always a bad idea for a waltz. Once 'The Waltz King' had consigned the words to the bin, however, the piece took off and became the most celebrated of all waltzes. It also made Strauss a very rich man.

As the musicians assembled to perform a new piano concerto, the Holy Roman Emperor Joseph II (1765–90) noticed that Mozart had composed a part for every player but himself. 'Where's your part?' he asked. Mozart tapped his forehead. 'In here.'

'Twelve notes in each octave and the varieties of rhythm offer me opportunities that all of human genius will never exhaust.'

IGOR STRAVINSKY (1882–1971)

[13]

'Composers are essentially a breed of men and women concerned with the arrangement of the same seven notes.'

RICHARD RODGERS (1902–79)

One day Rossini came across the Belgian music theorist François-Joseph Fétis (1784–1871). Fétis was carrying a copy of his own *Treatise on Counterpoint and Fugue*. Gesturing towards the volume, Rossini asked: 'Must all that be learned?' 'Not at all,' replied Fétis. 'You yourself are proof to the contrary.'

As he was scanning the shelves in a bookshop one day, Aaron Copland became aware of a woman buying a copy of his own book, *What to Listen for in Music*, together with a play by Shakespeare. As the woman began to pack the books in her bag, Copland went up to her and asked proudly: 'Would you like me to autograph your book?' Looking at the composer, the woman asked innocently: 'Which one?'

'The whole problem can be stated quite simply by asking, "Is there a meaning to music?" My answer to that would be, "Yes". And "Can you state in so many words what the meaning is?" My answer to that would be, "No".'

AARON COPLAND, *What to Listen for in Music* (1939)

Following the première of Aaron Copland's 'Symphony for organ' in 1925, conductor Walter Damrosch (1862–1950) remarked: 'If a young man at the age of twenty-three can write a symphony like that, in five years he will be ready to commit murder.'

'Among other observations, His Majesty [George III] said: "Dr Haydn, you have written a good deal." Haydn modestly replied: "Yes, Sire, a great deal more than is good." His Majesty neatly rejoined: "Oh, no, the world contradicts that."'

ADALBERT GYROWETZ, *Memoirs* (1848)

A contemporary once said of the Italian cellist and composer Luigi Boccherini (1743–1805), 'If God chose to speak to man he would employ the music of Haydn; but if he desired to hear an earthly musician, he would select Boccherini.'

Benjamin Britten on composing: 'I remember the first time I tried, the result looked rather like the Forth Bridge.'

Quoted in the *Sunday Telegraph* (1964)

Haydn on his early compositions: 'I thought then that everything was all right if only the paper was chock-full of notes.'

Quoted in Rosemary Hughes, *Haydn* (1950)

A young composer complained to Brahms about the
delay in the publication of his first work. 'Patience,'
Brahms advised. 'You can afford not to be immortal for
a few weeks more.'

One of the earliest works by the eccentric French
composer Erik Satie, *Vexations* (1893), is also one of
the shortest and longest piano pieces ever written.
Consisting of a few bars of music, the work carries the
instruction that it be played 840 times in succession.
The instruction was first carried out to the letter by a
group of musicians in New York in September 1963.
The marathon lasted eighteen hours and forty minutes.

'At the University of Leipzig ... Wagner majored in
gambling, duelling, drinking, and making love. When he
learned that he was supposed to attend classes too, he quit.'
    VICTOR BORGE, *My Favourite Intervals* (1974)

> It only irritated Brahms
> To tickle him under the arms.
> What really helped him compose
> Was to be stroked on the nose.

E. C. BENTLEY, *More Biography* (1929)

'Nothing primes inspiration more than necessity, whether
it be the presence of a copyist waiting for your work
or the prodding of an impresario tearing his hair. In my
time, all the impresarios in Italy were bald at thirty.
    I composed the overture to *Otello* in a little room
in the Barbaja palace wherein the baldest and fiercest of

directors had forcibly locked me with a lone plate of spaghetti and the threat that I would not be allowed to leave the room alive until I had written the last note.

I wrote the overture to *La Gazza Ladra* ['The Thieving Magpie'] the day of its opening in the theatre itself, where I was imprisoned by the director and under the surveillance of four stagehands who were instructed to throw my original text through the window, page by page, to the copyists waiting below to transcribe it. In default of pages, they were ordered to throw me out of the window bodily.

I did better with *The Barber*. I did not compose an overture, but selected for it one which was meant for a semi-serious opera called *Elisabetta*. The public was completely satisfied. I composed the overture to *Comte Ory* while fishing, with my feet in the water, and in the company of Signor Agnado who talked of Spanish finance. The overture for *William Tell* was composed under more or less similar circumstances. And as for *Mosè*, I did not write one.'

GIOACHINO ROSSINI, to an unknown correspondent; quoted in *Chambers Music Quotations* (1991)

According to legend, Rossini wrote *The Barber of Seville* (1816) in thirteen days – in his dressing gown and unshaven. Hearing about this, a friend remarked: 'How ironic that you should write *The Barber* without shaving.' 'If I had shaved,' protested Rossini, 'I would have gone out. And if I had gone out, I would not have come back in time to finish *The Barber* in thirteen days!'

Sir Charles Hallé once asked Donizetti if it was
true that Rossini had written *The Barber of Seville* in a
fortnight. '"Oh, I quite believe it," answered Donizetti.
"He was always such a lazy fellow!" I confess that
I looked with wonder and admiration at a man who
considered that to spend a whole fortnight over the
composition of an opera was a waste of time.'

Eager to lay his hands on Stravinsky's latest composition,
his publisher urged him to hurry up and finish it.
'Hurry!' roared the composer. 'I never hurry. I have no
time to hurry.'

During one of his journeys, Mozart was the guest of
a musician whose son, a boy of twelve, already played
the piano very skilfully. The boy told Mozart: 'I want
to compose something. How am I to begin?' Mozart
told him he was young and should wait. 'But,' the
boy protested, 'you were composing long before you
were my age.' 'True,' agreed Mozart, 'but I didn't have
to ask how to do it.' Seeing the boy downcast and
ashamed, Mozart added, 'If one has the spirit of a
composer, one writes because one cannot help it.' The
boy explained that he only wanted to know if Mozart
could recommend any book. 'All that is of no use,' the
composer told him. Then pointing to the boy's ear,
head, and heart, he said: 'Here, here, and here, is your
school. If all is right there, then you may take the pen
without delay.'

From Edward Holmes, *The Life of Mozart* (1845)

'The artist must regulate his life,' wrote the eccentric French composer Erik Satie, and in his *Memoirs of an Amnesiac*, he offers in this 'Musician's Day' (dated 15 February 1913), 'the precise time-table of my daily routine':

'I rise at 07.18; am inspired from 10.23 to 11.47. I lunch at 12.11 and leave the table at 12.14.

A healthy horseride round my estate from 13.19 to 14.53. Another inspiration from 15.12 to 16.07.

From 16.21 to 18.47 various occupations (fencing, reflection, immobility, visits, contemplation, dexterity, swimming, etc. . . .)

Dinner is served at 19.16 and finished at 19.20. Symphonic readings out loud, from 20.09 to 21.59.

I go to bed regularly at 22.37. Once a week I awake with a start at 03.14 (on Tuesdays). I eat only white food: eggs, sugar, shredded bones, the fat of dead animals, veal, salt, coconuts, chicken cooked in white water, mouldy fruit, rice, turnips, black pudding in camphor, pastry, cheese (white), cotton salad, and certain kinds of fish (skinless).

I boil my wine and drink it cold with the juice of the fuchsia. I have a good appetite, but never talk while eating for fear of strangling myself.

I breathe carefully (a little at a time). I dance very rarely. When walking I hold my sides and look steadily behind me. My expression is very serious; if I laugh it is unintentional. I always apologise very affably.

I sleep with only one eye; my sleep is very deep. My bed is round with a hole in it for my head to go through. Every hour a servant takes my temperature and gives me another. For a long time I have subscribed to a fashion magazine.

I wear a white bonnet, white stockings and a white waistcoat.

My doctor has always told me to smoke. His advice: "Smoke, my friend; if you don't, someone else will." '

When someone asked Rossini who was the greatest musician, the composer immediately replied: 'Beethoven.' 'But what about Mozart?' 'Oh, Mozart is not the *greatest*,' Rossini said, 'he is the *only*.'

'Working with you, Giacomo, is living in hell. Even the patience of Job could not endure such torment.'

LUIGI ILLICA (1857–1919), one of Puccini's librettists on *La Bohème*, *Tosca*, and *Madama Butterfly*; quoted in Arthur M. Abell, *Talks with Great Composers* (1955)

Sir Thomas Beecham on J. S. Bach: 'Too much counterpoint; what is worse, Protestant counterpoint.'

I would not go four miles to visit Sebastian Bach – or Batch – which is it?

CHARLES LAMB, *Free Thoughts on Several Eminent Composers* (1830)

In 1944, Stravinsky was commissioned to write a ballet for Anton Dolin and Alicia Markova in the Broadway show *The Seven Lively Arts*. After the first night, the producer Billy Rose cabled the composer: 'Ballet great success. Would be triumph if you reorchestrate it.' Stravinsky cabled back: 'Satisfied with great success.'

'For the Russians, I am a German, for the Germans, a Russian, for the classicists, I am futuristic, for the futurists, a reactionary. Conclusion: I am neither fish nor flesh, a deplorable individual.'

ANTON RUBINSTEIN (1829–94)

'It would be a serious error to consider Rubinstein a Russian composer. He is merely a Russian who composes.'

CESAR CUI; quoted in Jeremy Nicholas, *The Classic FM Guide to Classical Music* (1996)

[Cui's remark may have been sour grapes. As a member of the group of Russian composers known as 'The Five' or 'The Mighty Handful' (the others were Balakirev, Borodin, Mussorgsky, and Rimsky-Korsakov), Cui was the least significant.]

'Rimsky-Korsakov – what a name! It suggests fierce whiskers stained with vodka!'

Musical Courier (27 October 1897)

In 1876, French poet Stéphane Mallarmé (1842–98) wrote a poem entitled *L'Après-midi d'un Faune* ('Afternoon of a Faun'). This in turn inspired Debussy to write his *Prélude*. Mallarmé was not impressed: 'I would soon lose my voice if I went round roaring vacuously like a faun celebrating its afternoon.'

Critic's Choice

'Debussy's *L'Après-midi d'un Faune* was a strong example of modern ugliness. The faun must have had a terrible afternoon, for the poor beast brayed on muted horns and whinnied on flutes, and avoided all trace of soothing melody, until the audience began to share his sorrows.'

> LOUIS ELSON, *Daily Advertiser*, Boston (25 February 1904); quoted in Nicolas Slonimsky, *Lexicon of Musical Invective* (1965)

[Elson's opinion did not mellow with time. The following January he wrote again in the *Advertiser* in a similar vein: 'We cannot feel that all this extreme ecstasy is natural; it seems forced and hysterical; it is musical absinthe; there are moments when the suffering Faun in Debussy's *Afternoon of a Faun* seems to need a veterinary surgeon.']

'Edward Elgar, the figure head of music in England, is a composer whose rank it is neither prudent nor indeed possible to determine. Either it is one so high that only time and posterity can confer it, or else he is one of the Seven Humbugs of Christendom.'

GEORGE BERNARD SHAW, *Music and Letters* (1920)

Adele Strauss, the third wife of Johann Strauss II, one
day introduced her husband to the other great Viennese
composer of the day, Johannes Brahms. Although very
different in style, both composers respected and admired
each other, and they became firm friends. One story
goes that on their first meeting, Strauss handed Brahms
his autograph book and asked if he would do him the
honour of signing it. Brahms opened the book, chose a
blank page, neatly jotted down the opening bars of *The
Blue Danube*, and then wrote underneath: 'Unfortunately,
not by Johannes Brahms.'
[This story is also told of Brahms jotting the music and
inscription on the fan that Frau Strauss was carrying. Either
way, it's an impressive compliment.]

Nietzsche one day remarked to Wagner that in *The
Marriage of Figaro* Mozart had invented the music of
intrigue. Wagner replied: 'On the contrary! In *Figaro*
Mozart dissolved the intrigue in music.'

'Beethoven always sounds to me like the upsetting
of bags of nails, with here and there an also dropped
hammer.'

> JOHN RUSKIN; letter (6 February 1881); quoted in *The
> Guinness Dictionary of Poisonous Quotes* (1991)

When the conductor Hans von Bülow was asked to
name his favourite key, he replied: 'E flat.' His reason?
'It is the key of Beethoven's "Eroica" Symphony, and

has three ♭s in the key signature – one for Bach, one for Beethoven, one for Brahms.'

Arthur Sullivan, the composing half of Gilbert and Sullivan, returned home one night in such a merry state that he found it difficult to identify his front door from all the others in the terraced row. Fortunately, even when inebriated, Sullivan was blessed with excellent tonal sense. He walked along the row, pausing to kick the metal shoe scraper that stood outside each house. Finally, he found one that sounded familiar. He kicked it again. 'E flat! That's it!' he said, and let himself in.

The Russian composer of *Polovtzian Dances* and *On the Steppes of Central Asia*, Alexander Borodin (1833–87) once wrote that music 'is a relaxation from more serious occupations'. The latter included his work as an eminent scientist. His first published work was a paper entitled 'On the Action of Ethyl Iodide on Hydrobenzamide and Amarine'.

Borodin was once called as an expert witness in the case of two young and unknown composers, who were accusing each other of plagiarism. After listening to both compositions, Borodin was asked who was the injured party. He replied, 'My friend Mussorgsky.'

Critic's Choice

'*Une Nuit sur le Mont Chauve* ("Night on the Bare Mountain")
by Moussorgsky is as hideous a thing as we have ever
heard ... an orgy of ugliness and an abomination. May
we never hear it again!'

Musical Times, London (March 1898); quoted in Nicolas
Slonimsky, *Lexicon of Musical Invective* (1965)

According to legend, Charles Gounod's memory was
phenomenal. When he was twenty-one he watched and
listened to Berlioz directing a rehearsal of his latest
choral work *Roméo et Juliette*, which at the time was still
only in manuscript. The following morning Gounod
visited Berlioz, sat at the piano and proceeded to play
the entire last half of the work from memory. From the
very first notes, Berlioz stared at him in amazement,
touched with not a little anger and suspicion. Had
someone stolen the work? Had he unwittingly stolen
the work from someone else? 'Where the devil did you
get that music?' he demanded at last. 'At your rehearsal
yesterday,' replied Gounod.

A young man presented Cherubini with a score which
he said was by Étienne Méhul (1763–1817). 'This isn't
Méhul's work,' Cherubini said, after studying it. 'What
makes you say that?' asked the young man. 'It's not good
enough,' said Cherubini. 'Well, actually,' said the young
man, 'it's mine.' 'Rubbish,' Cherubini replied, 'it's too
good for you.'

A disgruntled composer with little talent marched into Cherubini's room one day brandishing the score of Rossini's latest success, *Mosè*. 'What do you say to this shocking thing by that libertine Rossini?' he seethed. 'It's a crime against music!' Cherubini replied: 'I wish I had committed it.'

'Give me a laundry-list and I will set it to music.'

> Attributed to ROSSINI; quoted in *The Treasury of Humorous Quotations* (1951)

'Rossini used to wear two or three wigs, one on top of the other, so he wouldn't have to bother taking the bottom one off.'

> VICTOR BORGE, *My Favourite Intervals* (1974)

Rossini was out walking with a friend, when he bumped into his rival, Giacomo Meyerbeer. Meyerbeer inquired after his health, and Rossini duly reeled off a list of ailments. Meyerbeer commiserated, wished him better, and went on his way. As soon as he was out of earshot, Rossini's friend seized his arm. 'I had no idea you had such problems,' he said, dreadfully concerned. 'You should be home resting in bed!' 'Nonsense, my dear chap,' replied Rossini, 'I'm as well as can be.' 'But you just said——' the friend exclaimed. 'Oh, that,' said Rossini. 'It will make Meyerbeer so happy to believe that I'm at death's door, and who am I to disappoint him?'

Meeting Stravinsky in the street one day, a gushing
lady shook his hand and thanked him for his music,
especially for her favourite *Scheherazade*. 'But no, madame,'
said Stravinsky, 'I did not compose *Scheherazade*'. 'Come,
come,' said the lady, 'don't be so modest.'

'A good melody is such a one as would grind about the
streets upon the organ.'

>   THOMAS ARNE (1710–78); quoted in Michael Kelly,
>   *Reminiscences* (1826)

Mascagni was hard at work on a new score one day
when an organ-grinder parked himself right underneath
his window and began an excerpt from the composer's
success *Cavalleria Rusticana* at completely the wrong
tempo. Irritated by the slowness, Mascagni rushed
out of the house and into the street. 'Here!' he cried,
seizing the handle from the organ-grinder, 'I am Pietro
Mascagni, and if you must play my music I must show
you how to play it correctly.' And so he did, till both
the composer and the street-musician were satisfied. The
following day the barrel organ returned, and Mascagni,
hearing his work played properly, looked out to see a
sign on the organ that read: 'Pupil of Mascagni.'

Staying with barrel organs for a moment, here's one
concerning Meyerbeer. He too was hard at work when
an organ-grinder outside his study window began
grinding out – not Meyerbeer, which the composer

could willingly have tolerated – but pure Rossini. Meyerbeer summoned a servant and was about to give him a couple of francs to persuade the man to go and grind somewhere else, when he had an idea. 'Here's four francs,' he told the servant. 'Tell that organist they're his if he'll go and play my music outside Rossini's.' The servant departed, and then returned. 'I'm sorry, Monsieur,' he said, 'but he refused.' 'Refused four francs?' asked Meyerbeer. 'Yes,' the servant replied. 'He says Rossini paid him eight francs – to play for you!'

'It may be a good thing to copy reality; but to invent reality is much, much better.'

> GIUSEPPE VERDI; letter (1876); quoted in *Chambers Music Quotations* (1991)

By the late 1870s, Verdi had created *Rigoletto, Il Trovatore, La Traviata, Aida,* and a number of other operatic heavyweights. Now he began to think seriously of writing what he'd been wanting to write for a long time: a comic opera. He probably would have written one too, if an article had not appeared just then in the *Gazetta musicale* quoting Rossini's opinion that Verdi had no gift for comedy. Verdi was furious, not least because the publisher of the *Gazetta,* Ricordi, was also his own publisher. 'For twenty years,' he wrote to Ricordi, 'I've been searching for a comic-opera libretto, and now that I've almost decided on one, you've persuaded the public to hiss it before it's even written! But never fear! If by chance – despite this Solemn Judgment – my evil genius persuades me to write a comic opera, then I'll let it ruin some other publisher!'

Reviewing a Boston Symphony concert conducted by Wilhelm Gericke (1845–1925), the critic of the *Boston Transcript* wrote: 'When Mr Gericke takes up his baton and commences to conduct a Brahms symphony, I have to weep for joy.' In response, Philip Hale, the leading music critic of the *Boston Herald* wrote: 'So do I have to weep, but not for joy, if it is in four movements and I am not sitting near the door.'

As you may guess from the above, Philip Hale was not an admirer of Brahms. On another occasion he wrote in the *Herald*: 'Someone should request manager Ellis to have a special door built in Symphony Hall with a sign over it in large red letters: "Emergency Exit, in case of Brahms".'

'Napoleon: "My dear Cherubini, you are certainly an excellent musician; but really your music is so noisy and complicated that I can make nothing of it."
Cherubini: "My dear general, you are certainly an excellent soldier; but, in regard to music, you must excuse me if I don't think it necessary to adapt my compositions to your comprehension."'

    LUIGI CHERUBINI; quoted in Edward Bellasis, *Cherubini: Memorials Illustrative of his Life* (1847)

Debussy was noted for being irritable and quarrelsome, so when the young Hungarian composer Béla Bartók, newly arrived in Paris, was offered the opportunity to meet anyone in the musical world who was anyone, it was thought odd that he should choose Debussy. 'What about Saint-Saëns?' asked his hosts. 'Or Widor?' Bartók stuck to his choice: Debussy. His hosts persisted: 'But he's such a dreadful man, and he'll almost certainly be rude and insult you. Surely you don't want that, do you?' 'Yes,' said Bartók.

Critic's Choice

'It is one's duty to hate with all possible fervor the empty and ugly in art; and I hate Saint-Saëns the composer with a hate that is perfect.'

J. F. RUNCIMAN, *Saturday Review*, London (12 December 1896); quoted in *They Got it Wrong: The Guinness Dictionary of Regrettable Quotations* (1993)

Hans von Bülow about Mahler's Second Symphony: 'If that was music, I no longer understand anything about the subject.'

Some appraisals are worth quoting for their sheer invention, and with this letter about Béla Bartók's Fourth Quartet, written by the Scottish critic and writer Alan Dent (1905–78) to fellow critic James Agate in November 1945 you certainly get your money's worth:
  'The opening Allegro took me straight back to childhood and gave me in turn the rusty windlass of

a well, the interlinking noises of a goods train that is being shunted, then the belly-rumblings of a little boy acutely ill after a raid on an orchard, and finally the singular alarmed noise of poultry being worried to death by a Scotch terrier.

The second movement gave me continuously and throughout its short length the noise of a November wind in telegraph poles on a lonely country road.

The third movement began with a dog howling at midnight, proceeded to imitate the regurgitations of the less-refined or lower middle-class type of water-closet cistern, modulating thence into the mass snoring of a Naval dormitory around the dawn – and concluded inconsequently with the cello reproducing the screech of an ungreased wheelbarrow.

The fourth movement took me straight back to the noises I made myself, on wet days indoors, at the age of six, by stretching and plucking a piece of elastic.

And the fifth movement reminded me immediately and persistently and vividly of something I have never thought of since the only time I heard it: the noise of a Zulu village in the Glasgow Exhibition – a hubbub all the more singular, because it had a background of skirling Highland bagpipes. Both noises emerged in this final movement of this Fourth Quartet of Béla Bartók.'

One of Sir Malcolm Arnold's more unconventional compositions was the piece he wrote for Gerard Hoffnung's Music Festival of 1956. Titled *A Grand, Grand Overture*, it was scored for full orchestra, four rifles, three vacuum cleaners and a floor polisher.

'If Master Korngold could make such a noise at fourteen, what will he not do when he is twenty-eight? The thought is appalling.'

A critic reviewing *Schauspiel-Ouvertüre* (1911), Erich Korngold's first orchestral work

'There is a definite limit to the length of time a composer can go on writing in one dance rhythm. This limit is obviously reached by Ravel toward the end of *La Valse* and toward the beginning of *Boléro*.'

Constant Lambert, *Music Ho!* (1934)

Critic's Choice

Ravel's *Boléro* I submit as the most insolent monstrosity ever perpetrated in the history of music. From the beginning to the end of its 339 measures it is simply the incredible repetition of the same rhythm and above all it is the blatant recurrence of an overwhelmingly vulgar cabaret tune that is little removed from the wail of an obstreperous back-alley cat.

Edward Robinson, *The American Mercury*, New York (May 1932)

'When I had completed my string quartet, Schoenberg turned grimly to me. "At the first playing," he said, "you will feel desperate."

I wasn't in Toronto when it was performed by the Kolisch Quartet, but they sent me the review, which went, "The Kolisch Quartet played last night at — Hall. Present at the concert were —." It went on to describe the guest list. That was the review.'

Oscar Levant, *The Memoirs of an Amnesiac* (1966)

'In former times no publisher or conductor would even go to the trouble of reading my music. Now that I am a famous and terrifying music critic, they are all eager to publish and to play. They still don't bother to read it.'

US composer Virgil Thomson (1896–1989), who became critic for the *New York Herald Tribune* in 1940

In 1892, Erik Satie collaborated with the poet J. P. Contamine de Latour on a three-act ballet called *Uspud*. In December that year, he submitted the manuscript to the Paris Opéra, but when the Director failed to acknowledge the receipt of it, Satie became so angry that he sent his seconds to the Opéra and challenged the Director to a duel! Although the affair was settled without the anticipated bloodshed, *Uspud* still received no production. Satie, however, was never one to waste an opportunity, and three years later he and the poet published the text and musical extracts from the ballet – together with an announcement on the cover that *Uspud* had been 'presented' at the Opéra on 20 December 1892.

When Archduke Ferdinand was considering employing the sixteen-year-old Wolfgang Amadeus Mozart as court musician in 1771, he wrote to his mother Maria Theresa (1717–80) for advice. She replied: 'You ask my opinion about taking the young Salzburg musician into your service. I do not know where you can place him, since I feel that you do not require a composer, or other useless people. But if it would give you pleasure, I have no wish to prevent you. What I say here is only meant to persuade you not to load yourself down with people who are useless, and to urge you not to give such people the right to represent themselves as being in your service. It gives one's service a bad name when such types run about like beggars; besides, he has a large family.'

Handel was not above the odd 'borrowing' from other composers, and being quite shameless about it too. Accused on one occasion of such a borrowing from his rival Giovanni Bononcini (whose operas were often more successful than his), Handel openly admitted it, and then as if to justify himself, said: 'It's much too good for him; he did not know what to do with it.'

Following a royal command performance of Mozart's *Die Entführung aus dem Serail* ('The Abduction from the Seraglio') on 16 July 1782, the Emperor, Joseph II, gave his judgment: 'Too fine for our ears, my dear Mozart,' he said, 'and much too many notes.' To this, Mozart replied: 'Exactly as many notes as are necessary, your Majesty.'

'Whether the angels play only Bach praising God, I am not quite sure. I am sure however that *en famille* they play Mozart.'

KARL BARTH (1886–1968), Swiss theologian; quoted in his *New York Times* obituary (11 December 1968)

'If I were a dictator, I should make it compulsory for every member of the population between the ages of four and eighty to listen to Mozart for at least a quarter of an hour daily for the coming five years.'

SIR THOMAS BEECHAM; quoted in Harold Atkins and Archie Newman, *Beecham Stories* (1978)

When Gershwin asked Arnold Schoenberg to accept him as a pupil, the inventor of twelve-note music replied: 'I would only make you a bad Schoenberg,' he explained, 'and you're such a good Gershwin already.'

Maurice Ravel also refused him, saying: 'You would only lose the spontaneous quality of your melody, and end by writing bad Ravel.'

An apocryphal story is also told that Gershwin went to Stravinsky with the same request. Stravinsky asked the American about his annual income, and when he heard that it was around $250,000, he replied: 'You teach me.'

In 1786, Beethoven, then a youth just entering on his musical career, came on a visit to Vienna. There he was introduced to Mozart, and for a short time became his pupil. Mozart gave Beethoven a piece to extemporise upon, and while he was working on it, said to some persons, who were standing near him in an adjoining apartment: 'Listen to that young man; he will some day make a noise in the world.'

From Edward Holmes, *The Life of Mozart* (1845)

'On my word of honour, I have never felt such self-satisfaction, such pride, such happiness, as in the knowledge that I have created a good thing.'

TCHAIKOVSKY; letter to his publisher Pyotr Jürgenson in August 1893, on his Sixth Symphony ('Pathétique')

Critic's Choice

'The Pathétique Symphony threads all the foul ditches and sewers of human despair; it is as unclean as music well can be.'

W. F. APTHORP, Boston *Evening Transcript* (31 October 1898); quoted in Nicolas Slonimsky, *Lexicon of Musical Invective* (1965)

'Female admirer: "How do you think of those lovely
melodies?"
Gounod: "God, Madame, sends me down some of
his angels and they whisper sweet melodies in my ear."'
  Quoted in James Harding, *Gounod* (1973)

In his autobiography, *World Within World*, Stephen Spender
tells about the time Virginia and Leonard Woolf invited
the elderly English composer Dame Ethel Smyth to
dinner at their house at Rodmell in Sussex: 'Dame Ethel
bicycled the twenty miles from the village where she lived
to Rodmell, dressed in rough tweeds. About two miles
from her destination she decided that perhaps she was
not suitably dressed for a dinner party. She thought that
possibly corsets were required to smarten up her figure.
Accordingly, she went into a village shop and asked for
some corsets. There were none. Distressed, she looked
around the shop and her eye lighted on a bird cage,
which she purchased. About twenty minutes later, Virginia
went into her garden to discover Dame Ethel in a state
of undress in the shrubbery struggling with the bird cage,
which she was wrenching into the shape of corsets and
forcing under her tweeds.'

'Beethoven esteemed Mozart and Handel most of
all composers, and next to them Sebastian Bach.
If ever I found him with music in his hand, or
on his desk, it was sure to be that of one of these
mighty men.'
  ANTON SCHINDLER, *Life of Beethoven* (1840)

'A certain count in Prague had requested Mozart to write some "country-dances", and had been promised them, but they were not forthcoming. The count had recourse to a trick. He invited the composer to dinner, informing him that on this occasion it would be served an hour earlier than usual. On his arrival at the appointed time, the master of the house ordered the necessary writing materials to be brought, and pressed him to fulfil his promise for a ball that was to take place on the following day. Thus ungenerously entrapped, Mozart set to work, and in less than half an hour was ready with four country-dances for a full orchestra.'

EDWARD HOLMES, *The Life of Mozart* (1845)

'There is a curious English musical dictionary, published in 1827, which may sometimes be found in the fourpenny box outside a second-hand bookshop; and in this dictionary Beethoven is given one of the largest articles and treated as unquestionably the greatest composer of the day (though on the evidence only of his less dangerous works). Such was Beethoven's fame in the year of his death. Schubert died in the next year. There are five Schuberts in this dictionary, but Franz Schubert is not among them.'

DONALD FRANCIS TOVEY (1875–1940), *Essays and Lectures on Music* (1927) 'Franz Schubert'

In these cost conscious 'value-for-money' days, is there really any room for labour-intensive musical works? Not according to this story of a company chairman who was given a ticket to a concert at which the main work on the programme was Schubert's 'Unfinished' Symphony. The chairman was unable to attend, so he passed on the invitation to the company's Director of Administration. Meeting the DA in the lift the following morning the chairman asked him if he had enjoyed the concert. One of the new school of effective management, the DA replied cryptically: 'You'll have my report by lunch.' Sure enough, before lunch the chairman received an immaculate document headed:

Report: Concert Attendance Wednesday 12.4.95 19.30–22.16
Subject: Symphony, Schubert – 'Unfinished', No.8 in B minor;
efficiency thereof

(a) For considerable periods the four oboe players had nothing to do. The number should be reduced, and their workload redistributed throughout the orchestra. In this way, peaks of inactivity would be eliminated.

(b) All twelve violins were playing identical notes. This is unnecessary duplication; the personnel of this section should also be reduced. If a large volume of sound is required this may be obtained at considerably less expense by means of computer technology.

(c) Too much effort was expended in the playing of demi-semiquavers: an excessive and unnecessary refinement. It is therefore recommended that all notes be rounded up to the nearest semiquaver. This done, it should be possible to use 'work experience' students and other casuals.

(d) The repetition with horns of passages already played by the strings is superfluous and serves no purpose. The elimination of all such redundant passages throughout the programme would reduce the concert's running time from two hours to twenty minutes.

Conclusion: If Schubert had implemented the above in the first place, he would doubtless have finished his symphony.

One of the most celebrated pieces of the American modernistic composer George Antheil (1900–59) is *Ballet Mécanique* (1924). The piece is scored for ten grand pianos, six xylophones, four bass drums, together with an odd variety of unorthodox instruments, including two octaves of electric bells, several klaxons, anvils and power-driven saws, a fire-alarm and even an airplane propeller. Understandably, at its first American performance at Carnegie Hall, some of the audience were shocked, some were amused, and some even amazed. For one concertgoer in the front row, however, the experience was just too much. Less than ten minutes after the performance began, he tied a handkerchief to his cane and raised the white flag in surrender.

'Composers should write tunes that chauffeurs and errand boys can whistle.'

SIR THOMAS BEECHAM; quoted in the *New York Times* (9 March 1961)

In 1904, Richard Strauss began a one-act opera based on Oscar Wilde's play *Salome*. Following its first production in Dresden in December 1905, there were accusations of blasphemy and battles with the censor. Kaiser Wilhelm II (1859–1941) is said to have commented, 'I really like

this fellow Strauss, but *Salome* will do him a lot of harm.'
In spite of this, the opera was highly successful (over the
next two years it was performed at fifty opera houses),
and gave Strauss a healthy income. Reminded of the
Kaiser's remark about doing him a lot of harm, he
commented, 'I was able to build my villa in Garmisch,
thanks to the harm.'

'His absurd cacophony will not be music even in the
thirtieth century.'

CESAR CUI about the music of Richard Strauss; letter
(1904)

Eduard Lassen, the composer and conductor of the
Weimar Opera, once told Richard Strauss: 'This
Wagner craze is only a passing phenomenon, and fifty
years from now he will be forgotten. His music is noisy,
vulgar and blatant, and in due time he will find his true
place in musical history.' 'He certainly will,' Strauss
replied. 'In fifty years he will rank as the greatest of all
composers of opera.'

'I like Wagner's music better than anybody's. It is so
loud that one can talk the whole time without people
hearing what one says. That is a great advantage.'

OSCAR WILDE, *The Picture of Dorian Gray* (1891)

Strauss once complained to Paul Hindemith about the
young composer's savage anti-Romantic scores: 'Why
do you write this way? You have talent.' Hindemith

replied: 'Herr Professor, you make your music and I'll make mine.' On another occasion, having listened to Hindemith's latest composition, Strauss asked him how long it had taken him to write it. 'About three days,' replied Hindemith. 'Yes,' said Strauss sadly, 'that's exactly what I thought!'

'I may not be a first-rate composer, but I am a first-class second-rate composer!'

> RICHARD STRAUSS; quoted in Norman Del Mar, *Richard Strauss* (1962)

Asked if he was a Wagnerian or a Brahmsian, Richard Strauss replied: 'I am a a Selfian.'

When the Russian composer Alexander Scriabin (1872–1915) arrived in Paris to give a concert, he was still virtually unknown. He was therefore delighted to meet the young pianist Arthur Rubinstein, who was not only a great admirer of Scriabin's music but could also speak his language. Scriabin immediately invited the young pianist to join him for tea, and the two went immediately to a nearby fashionable café. When they were settled and had given their order, Scriabin asked: 'Who is your favourite composer?' Without a moment's hesitation the young pianist answered: 'Brahms.' This was clearly not the right answer for Scriabin. He leapt out of his seat, and banged his fist on the table. 'What! What?' he screamed. 'How can you like that dreadful composer and me at the same time? When I was your age I was a Chopinist, later I became a Wagnerite, but now I can be only a Scriabinist!' And in a rage, he stormed out of the café, leaving a stunned Rubinstein to pay the bill.

'If it must be Richard, I prefer Wagner; if it must be Strauss, I prefer Johann.'

ANON; quoted in *The Guinness Dictionary of Poisonous Quotes* (1991)

'The material of music is sound and silence. Integrating these is composing.'

JOHN CAGE, *Silence* (1961); quoted in *Cassell Companion to 20th-century Music* (1997)

One of the most unusual – and quietest – pieces of music ever written is *4′ 33″* by the experimental composer John Cage (1912–92). The title refers to the four minutes and thirty-three seconds the piece lasts, though the only way of telling that is by a stopwatch. Composed in 1952, the piece consists of silent music. It has a blank score with time signatures and the key, but no notes, only rests, and it can be performed by anyone on any instrument or group of instruments, and in any way. In the past, it has most commonly been performed by a pianist, who indicates by gestures that the work is in three movements, and then sits motionless for the allotted time. The end of the piece is most apparent when the pianist lowers the piano lid and departs.

Hearing about 4'33", Stravinsky remarked that he was looking forward to a full-length work by the same composer.

'It is better to make a piece of music than to perform one, better to perform one than to listen to one, better to listen to one than to misuse it as a means of distraction, entertainment, or acquisition of "culture".'

> JOHN CAGE, 'Forerunners of Modern Music; At Random'
> in *Tiger's Eye* (March 1949)

'After silence, that which comes nearest to expressing the inexpressible is music.'

> ALDOUS HUXLEY, *Music at Night* (1931)

'I liked your opera. I think I will set it to music.'

> LUDWIG VAN BEETHOVEN, to a fellow but lesser composer

When the English pianist, and founder-member of the Royal Philharmonic Society, Charles Neate (1784–1877), visited Beethoven in 1815, he tried to persuade the composer to return with him to England for expert treatment for his deafness. Beethoven refused. 'I have already had all sorts of medical advice. I shall never be cured,' he said, and then proceeded to tell Neate how

he went deaf. 'I was once busy writing an opera ...
no, it was not *Fidelio*. I had a very ill-tempered *primo
tenore* [leading tenor] to deal with. I had already written
two grand airs to the same text, with which he was
dissatisfied, and now a third, which upon trial, he
seemed to approve and took away with him. I thanked
the stars that I was at length rid of him and sat down
immediately to a work which I had laid aside for those
airs and which I was anxious to finish. I had not been
half an hour at my work when I heard a knock at my
door which I immediately recognised as that of my
primo tenore. I sprang up from my table under such an
excitement of rage that as the man entered the room
I threw myself upon the floor as they do on the stage,
coming down on my hands. When I arose I found
myself deaf and have been so ever since. The physicians
say the nerve is injured.'

'A nation creates music – the composer only arranges it.'
    MIKHAIL GLINKA; quoted in *Theatre Arts Magazine*, New
    York (June 1958)

'Composing a piece of music is very feminine. It is
sensitive, emotional, contemplative. By comparison,
doing housework is positively masculine.'
    US composer BARBARA KOLB (born 1939);
    quoted in *Time* (10 November 1975)

'From about age eight I had the idea I wanted to be a

composer – mainly, at that time, in order to become very, very famous.'

> Canadian composer and teacher JOHN BECKWITH (born 1927); interviewed in *Musicanada* (November 1967)

'Delius is all intoxication but it is all the same intoxication. Wagner has a hundred ways of making you tight.'

> ANON; quoted by James Agate in *Ego* 7 (17 September 1944)

'Is Wagner a human being at all? Is he not rather a disease? He contaminates everything he touches – he has made music sick. I postulate this viewpoint: Wagner's art is diseased.'

> FRIEDRICH NIETZSCHE, *Der Fall Wagner*; quoted in *They Got it Wrong: The Guinness Dictionary of Regrettable Quotations* (1995)

> A friend said to Chopin
> It would be topin
> If only yude
> Write an étude.

> ANON; quoted in *Handbook of 20th Century Quotations* (1984)

The evening before the first performance of *Don Giovanni*, Mozart was reminded that he still had not written the overture. Finally, at midnight, he retired to his apartment and began to work. Soon, however, he fell asleep. His wife Constanze tried to wake him, but it was hopeless, and in the end she let him stay asleep till five o'clock in the morning, only two hours before the music-copiers arrived at seven. Nevertheless, by the time they did come, the overture was finished.

The copiers were slower than expected, and though the opera should have commenced at seven in the evening, there was still no overture, and the crowded theatre was kept waiting until a quarter to eight, when the parts were hastily brought into the orchestra, and with them entered Mozart to take his place as conductor. His appearance was greeted by the general applause of the theatre, and the unrehearsed overture was then commenced.

During its performance the audience gave many signs of repressed pleasure, which at length broke out into a loud exclamation. When the curtain rose and the first scene of the opera was going forward, Mozart said to some of the musicians near him, 'The overture went off very well on the whole, although a good many notes certainly fell under the desks.'

From Edward Holmes, *The Life of Mozart* (1845)

'It is not hard to compose, but it is wonderfully hard to let the superfluous notes fall under the table.'

J. S. BACH; quoted by Dudley Moore, *Off-beat* (1986)

'I shall gain but little by this; but I have pleased myself, that must be my recompense.'

MOZART, after he completed writing *The Marriage of Figaro*; quoted in Edward Holmes, *The Life of Mozart* (1845)

Not everyone, of course, is a fan of Mozart. The outspoken and unorthodox Canadian pianist Glenn Gould (1932–82) once said of Mozart's Symphony in G minor: 'The G-minor Symphony consists of eight remarkable measures – surrounded by a half-hour of banality.' According to *The Guinness Dictionary of Poisonous Quotes*, he also made the sacrilegious pronouncement: 'Mozart died too late rather than too soon.'

Critic's Choice

'The music of *The Love for Three Oranges*, I fear, is too much for this generation . . . Mr Prokofiev might well have loaded up a shotgun with several thousand notes of various lengths and discharged them against the side of a blank wall.'

EDWARD MOORE, *Chicago Tribune* (31 December 1921)

'It is a curious thing that the performances which I have hated and loathed as being a caricature of my thoughts are the very ones held up as patterns.'

SIR EDWARD ELGAR; quoted by Basil Maine, *Elgar: His Life and Works* (1933)

Brahms was not noted for his tolerance, particularly where the name of Wagner was concerned. According

to one tale, Brahms was visiting the conductor Hermann
Levi in Munich when, in the course of conversation, Levi
happened to mention Gluck and then Wagner in the same
connection. Brahms was furious. 'One doesn't pronounce
those two names like that, one after the other!' He dashed
from the room, and left Munich the following day.

'The Third Symphony is an example at the height of
music because the work gives no clue to what it means.
It is simply a piece of music.'
   SIR EDWARD ELGAR about Brahms's Third Symphony;
   quoted by Basil Maine, *Elgar: His Life and Works* (1933)

'Never compose anything unless the not composing of it
becomes a positive nuisance to you.'
   GUSTAV HOLST; letter (1921); quoted by Nat Shapiro,
   Encyclopedia of Quotations about Music (1978)

Critic's Choice
'The Finale of the Fourth Symphony of Tchaikovsky
pained me by its vulgarity ... Nothing can redeem the
lack of nobleness, the barbarous side, by which, according
to ethnographs and diplomats, even the most polished
Russian at times betrays himself.'
   Musical Review (26 February 1880)

When Offenbach (1819–80) dismissed his valet, he

provided him with such an impeccable reference that a prospective employer was naturally suspicious. Calling on Offenbach, he asked if the valet was really as good as the composer claimed, and if he was, why was he sacked. Offenbach assured the man that the valet was everything he described in the reference, except for one rather important factor. 'For you, he'll make an excellent valet, but for me as a composer, he doesn't do at all. You see, he used to beat my clothes outside my door every morning, and his tempo is non-existent.'

'There can no more be a new Beethoven than there can be a new Christopher Columbus.'

> RENÉ LEONORMOND, *Étude sur L'Harmonie Moderne* (1913)

'You can chase a Beethoven symphony all your life and never catch up.'

> ANDRÉ PREVIN; quoted by Nat Shapiro, *Encyclopedia of Quotations about Music* (1978)

Critic's Choice

'Opinions are divided concerning the merits of the 'Pastoral' Symphony of Beethoven, though very few venture to deny that it is much too long. The Andante alone is upwards of a quarter of an hour in performance, and, being a series of repetitions, might be subjected to abridgement without any violation of justice, either to the composer or his hearers.'

> *The Harmonicon*, London (June 1823)

'Beethoven's Fifth is the most sublime noise that has ever penetrated into the ear of man.'

E. M. FORSTER, *Howards End* (1910)

> The devil, with his foot so cloven,
> For aught I care may take Beethoven;
> And, if the bargain does not suit,
> I'll throw him Weber in to boot!

CHARLES LAMB, *Free Thoughts on Several Eminent Composers* (1830)

'I find that I never lose Bach. I don't know why I have always loved him so. Except that he is so pure, so relentless and incorruptible, like a principle of geometry.'

EDNA ST VINCENT MILLAY, *Letters* (1943)

Harry Angelo's *Reminiscences* (1828) cites the following conversation between Johann Sebastian Bach's youngest son Johann Christian (1735–82) and a colleague, the German musician Carl Friedrich Abel (1723–87). The conversation concerned the current talk of the town – a certain preacher, Dr Dodd, who had been condemned to death for fraud:

'The kind-hearted Abel, who was a libertine in his sentiments, insisted that a mere act of fraud ought not to be visited with the same dreadful penalty as that of the rascal assassin. Bach, though no less good hearted, asserted, rather too coldly and pertinaciously for the warm temper of Abel, that fraud was the act of a dirty mind. "What the devil do you talk of Doctor Dodd being in debt? Are not you sometimes in debt? Am not I always in debt? And is it proper and right, because of that, I am to commit forgery? I do insist upon it, my dear friend, Mister Abel, that he that commits forgery of notes, ought to be hanged. Such a man is a rogue, and not fit to live in society."

Abel, who was ever addicted to droning, instantly replied, "O! O! Master Bach! Well then, Sir, you and myself should be hanged; for have we not both of us forged notes enough in our times?"

"That is not kind of you, my dear Abel," said Bach. "To be sure, as you say, friend Abel, us composers are pirates and plagiarists, and forgers of notes. But," he added, with a sly look, "some composers forge false notes, and I only forge true.'"

'Of all the elements united in the performance of music, rhythm is the one most natural to us, as it is equally natural to all animals.'

JEAN-PHILIPPE RAMEAU (1683–1764), *Le Nouveau Système de Musique Théoretique* (1726)

Igor Stravinsky was once quoted as saying 'My music is best understood by children and animals'(*Observer*, 8 October 1961). Was he referring perhaps in part to one of the most bizarre commissions he ever accepted? It began with a call in 1942 from the choreographer George Balanchine (1904–83) who needed some music for a ballet he was going to choreograph for the Ringling Brothers, Barnum and Bailey Circus. Stravinsky asked him what sort of music he had in mind. Balanchine told him a polka, and then added: 'For elephants.' If Balanchine was expecting some expression of surprise from the composer, he was disappointed, for Stravinsky's next question was: 'How old?' When Balanchine told him: 'Young!' Stravinsky answered: 'Okay, if they're very young, I'll do it.' He did, too, and according to Balanchine, the resulting *Circus Polka* served its purpose very well with audiences and elephants alike 'on no less than 425 times'.

'I don't write modern music. I only write good music.'
    STRAVINSKY to journalists on his first visit to America in
    1925

'Tell me, Dr Vaughan Williams,' asked an American journalist when the elderly composer visited the United States, 'what do you think about music?' Vaughan Williams looked quizzically at the man for a moment, and then said: 'It's a rum go!'

Some composers are quite ambivalent about their compositions. Take, for instance, Vaughan Williams on a passage in his Fourth Symphony: 'It looks wrong, and it sounds wrong, but it's right.' Of the same symphony he also said once: 'I don't know if I like it, but it's what I meant.' On another occasion, after a performance of his Second Symphony ('A London Symphony'), he remarked: 'I realise now, it is not as boring as I thought it was.'

After attending the London Symphony Orchestra recording of his Sixth Symphony, Vaughan Williams commiserated with the players: 'It must be hell to play it for three hours. I know, it's been hell to listen to it.'

'I always seem to have a vague feeling that he [Beethoven] is a Satan among musicians, a fallen angel in the darkness who is perpetually seeking to fight his way back to happiness.'

British psychologist, HAVELOCK ELLIS (1859–1939), *Impressions and Comments* (1914); entry for 3 September 1913, referring to Beethoven

Critic's Choice

'We find Beethoven's Ninth Symphony to be precisely one hour and five minutes long; a fearful period indeed, which puts the muscles and lungs of the band, and the patience of the audience to a severe trial.'

The Harmonicon, London (April 1825)

'Beethoven impetuously threw himself at Cherubini's feet, explicitly and personally acknowledging him as his master; a compliment which poor Cherubini could return only by complaining that Beethoven's music made him sneeze.'

DONALD FRANCIS TOVEY (1875–1940), *Essays in Musical Analysis* IV (1937)

Beethoven's favourite composer, Cherubini, was said to be extremely meticulous. If ever he made a mistake on his manuscript, no matter how small, he would painstakingly cut out the area, and paste in a fresh piece of manuscript paper, with the result that some of his works, when finished, looked like a collage.

One of Cherubini's former pupils, Jacques Fromental Halévy (1799–1862), invited him to attend the première of his latest opera. After the first act, he asked Cherubini what he thought. Cherubini said nothing. After the second act, Halévy repeated the question. Again no answer. Finally, he could contain himself no longer. 'Maestro,' he said, 'have you nothing to say to me?' And Cherubini replied sadly: 'Why should I have? For two hours you have said nothing to me.'

Another of Cherubini's pupils was the prolific and – at the time – successful composer Daniel François Esprit Auber (1782–1871). Surprisingly, or perhaps not, Auber never attended a performance of any of his operas. 'If I did,' he said, 'I could never write another note.' However, he did enjoy the works of Rossini, and one evening very late in his life he went to hear *William Tell*. Sitting there expectantly for the pleasure of the cello trio which begins the overture, he was suddenly startled out of his mood of anticipation by a totally different sound – and what's worse it was something he himself had written. He immediately sought an explanation from an official. Due to the indisposition of one of the leading singers, the official told him, the management were unable to stage *William Tell* that evening, and in its place they were pleased to present instead Auber's *Masaniello*. Auber rushed from the theatre as fast as his aged legs would carry him.

Almost as bad as having to listen to his own works, was having to listen to other people's – especially those of the new generation of composers who displayed any kind of 'originality'. When a work by one such precocious youth was presented to him for appraisal, Auber commented sourly: 'This boy will go far, when he has had less experience.'

'The good composer is slowly discovered, the bad composer is slowly found out.'

> SIR ERNEST NEWMAN; quoted in *Chambers Music Quotations* (1991)

Some cry up Haydn, some Mozart,
Just as the whim bites. For my part,
I do not care a farthing candle
For either of them, or for Handel.

CHARLES LAMB, *Free Thoughts on Several Eminent Composers* (1830)

'Everything went right for Bizet until the day he
was born.'

VICTOR BORGE, *My Favourite Intervals* (1974)

Critic's Choice

'Brahms' *Requiem* has not the true funereal relish: it is so
execrably and ponderously dull that the very flattest of
funerals would seem like a ballet, or at least, a *danse
macabre*, after it.'

GEORGE BERNARD SHAW, *The World* (9 November 1892)

'Mozart has the classic purity of light and the blue
ocean; Beethoven the romantic grandeur which belongs
to the storms of air and sea, and while the soul
of Mozart seems to dwell on the ethereal peaks of
Olympus, that of Beethoven climbs shuddering the
storm-beaten sides of a Sinai. Blessed be they both! Each
represents a moment of the ideal life, each does us good.
Our love is due to both.'

Swiss philosopher HENRI-FREDERIC AMIEL (1821–81),
entry for 17 December 1856 in *Journal Intime* (1882)

'On 6 April 1822, Beethoven had inquired of his old pupil [Ferdinand Ries]: "What would the [Royal] Philharmonic Society be likely to offer me for a symphony?" Ries, evidently, laid the matter before the directors of the society who, at a meeting on 10 November "resolved to offer Beethoven fifty pounds for a MS symphony" ... Beethoven, although he protested that the remuneration was not to be compared with what other nations might give, accepted the offer, adding, "I would write gratis for the first artists of Europe if I were not still poor Beethoven. If I were in London, what would I not write for the Philharmonic Society! For Beethoven can write, God be thanked, though he can do nothing else in this world."'

> Quoted in ALEXANDER WHEELOCK THAYER (1817–97),
> *Life of Ludwig van Beethoven*, translated by Henry E. Krehbiel
> (1866–79)

'The aim and final end of all music should be none other than the glory of God and the refreshment of the soul. If heed is not paid to this, it is not true music but a diabolical bawling and twanging.'

> JOHANN SEBASTIAN BACH; quoted in *The Guinness Dictionary
> of Poisonous Quotes* (1991)

'I don't like composers who think. It gets in the way of their plagiarism.'

> Librettist HOWARD DIETZ (1896–1983)

'A good composer does not initiate, he steals.'

> IGOR STRAVINSKY; quoted in Peter Yates, *Twentieth Century
> Music* (1967)

Hone's *Table Book* of 1835 relates the following tale (which should perhaps — like so many of Hone's tales — be taken with a pinch of salt) about the English composer John Bull (?1562–1628):

'Dr. Bull hearing of a famous musician belonging to a certain cathedral at St. Omer's [France], he applied himself as a novice to him, to learn something of his faculty, and to see and admire his works. This musician, after some discourse had passed between them, conducted Bull to a vestry or music-school joining to the cathedral, and showed to him a lesson or song of forty parts, and then made a vaunting challenge to any person in the world to add one more part to them, supposing it to be so complete and full that it was impossible for any mortal man to correct or add to it; Bull thereupon desiring the use of pen, ink, and ruled paper, such as we call music paper, prayed the musician to lock him up in the said school for two or three hours; which being done, not without great disdain by the musician, Bull in that time, or less, added forty more parts to the said lesson or song. The musician thereupon being called in, he viewed it, tried it, and retried it; at length he burst out into a great ecstasy, and swore by the great God, that he that added those forty parts must either be the devil, or Dr. Bull ... Whereupon Bull making himself known, the musician fell down and adored him.'

Though full of great musical lore
Old Bach was a terrible bore
A fugue without a tune
He thought was a boon
So he wrote seventeen thousand more.

Musical Herald (1884)

'There is so much talk about music, and yet so little is said. For my part, I believe, that words do not suffice for such a purpose and if I find they did suffice, I would finally have nothing more to do with music.'

FELIX MENDELSSOHN; letter (1842); quoted in *Chambers Music Quotations* (1991)

'He snarled at everyone ... a dirty, foul, dark man.'

FRAU MEINANDER describing Beethoven; quoted in *The Guinness Dictionary of Poisonous Quotes* (1991)

'I must confess that I live a miserable life ... I live entirely in my music.'

LUDWIG VAN BEETHOVEN; letter (1801)

'I regard all pop music as irrelevant in the sense that people in 200 years won't be listening to what is being written and played today. I think they will be listening to Beethoven.'

ELTON JOHN (born 1947); quoted in KLM Magazine *Flagship* (March 1998)

'Ah Mozart! He was happily married – but his wife wasn't.'

VICTOR BORGE; quoted in *The Guinness Dictionary of Poisonous Quotes* (1991)

'It is sobering to consider that when Mozart was my age he had been dead a year.'

TOM LEHRER (born 1928); quoted in *Chambers Music Quotations* (1991)

'One morning a neat little gentleman came into [Howell's] shop and asked to look at some pianoforte music, and he [Howell] laid before him some sonatas by Haydn which had just been published. The stranger turned them over and said, "No, I don't like these." Howell replied, "Do you see they are by Haydn, Sir?" "Well, Sir, I do, but I wish for something better." "Better," cried Howell indignantly, "I am not anxious to serve a gentleman of your taste," and was turning away when the customer made it known that he was Haydn himself. Howell, in astonishment, embraced him and the composer was so flattered by the interview that a long and intimate friendship followed.'

WILLIAM GARDINER, *Music and Friends* (1838–53)

'Beethoven is about trying to get on with your wife. It is a reconciliation of opposites.'

SIR COLIN DAVIS (born 1927); quoted by Dudley Moore, *Off-beat* (1986)

'Except when deep in a piece of music that had to be finished by a certain date, Sullivan even welcomed the distraction of visitors while he was composing, and many of his melodies came to him in the noise and bustle of a social crush, when he would pull out a notebook and commit them to paper. He scored with great rapidity, smoking cigarette after cigarette and chatting without effort to the visitor of the moment. "Why, it's like writing shorthand," said George Grossmith after watching him for a moment in silence. "Yes, but it's much quicker," replied Sullivan.'

HESKETH PEARSON, *Gilbert and Sullivan* (1935)

An aspiring composer called on Rossini clutching two compositions he had recently finished. Would the great man listen to them both and say which he thought was the better? Against his better judgment, Rossini agreed to adjudicate. The young man sat at the piano and enthusiastically played through the first composition. Just as he finished it, Rossini held up his hand: 'You need not play any more,' he said. 'I prefer the second piece.'

'I like Toronto because nobody hates me here – unlike New York or Vienna.'

IGOR STRAVINSKY; quoted by John Kraglund in *The Globe and Mail* (6 May 1972)

'We ought to have books teaching us not how to compose music but how to decompose it.'

SAMUEL BUTLER, *Notebooks* (published 1912)

Brahms once took the most elaborate pains to play
a trick on the celebrated Beethoven scholar Gustav
Nottebohm (1817–82). Nottebohm often accompanied
Brahms on his evening stroll through the Viennese
streets, and usually bought his cold supper from a
certain cheese and sausage peddler. Brahms's friend
and biographer Max Kalbeck (1850–1921) relates
how one evening Nottebohm 'received his victuals
wrapped in old music paper covered with crabbed
notes, apparently in Beethoven's handwriting. Fighting
down his excitement, he marched to the next lamppost,
unfolded the paper, examined it carefully through his
spectacles, smoothed it, and without a word shoved
it into his pocket. The cheese he kept in his hand
and ate as he walked, assuring the others that he was
unusually hungry that day. And never did he drop a
syllable about his find – to the huge disappointment
of the company who had been let by Brahms into the
secret. For the mysterious sheet contained a variation
of the latest popular song-hit. That rascal Brahms had
fabricated it in masterly imitation of Beethoven's pen
scratches, and enjoined the peddler to wrap it around
the professor's cheese.'

'Mozart makes you believe in God – much more than
going to church – because it cannot be by chance that
such a phenomenon arrives into this world and then
passes after thirty-six years, leaving behind such an
unbounded number of unparalleled masterpieces.'

SIR GEORG SOLTI (1912–97)

[63]

'An atheistic upbringing is fatal. No atheist has ever created anything of great and lasting value.'

> WAGNER in conversation with Engelbert Humperdinck (1854–1921) in 1880; quoted in Arthur M. Abell, *Talks with Great Composers* (1955)

'I know several young composers who are atheists. I have read their scores, and I assure you, Joseph, that they are doomed to speedy oblivion, because they are utterly lacking in inspiration. Their works are purely cerebral ... No atheist has ever been or ever will be a great composer.'

> BRAHMS in conversation with the violinist Joseph Joachim (1831–1907) in 1896; quoted in Arthur M. Abell, *Talks with Great Composers* (1955)

[A Lady] 'being very musical, was invited ... to a private Rehearsal of the *Messiah*, and being struck with the Exceeding dignity of expression in the Chorusses, and other parts of ye oratorio so inimitably sett to the sacred words, after the musick was over she asked him [Handel] how it was possible for him who understood the English Language but imperfectly, to enter so fully into the sublime spirit of the Words. His answer is I think a lesson to all Composers, at least of Sacred Musick, "Madam, I thank God I have a little religion".'

> CHARLES BURNEY; letter (30 March 1776); quoted in William C. Smith, *A Handelian's Notebook* (1965)

On hearing Handel's 'Hallelujah' Chorus, Joseph Haydn said: 'He is the master of us all.'

  Quoted in Christopher Headington, *The Bodley Head History of Western Music* (1974)

'I sat close by [Beethoven] and heard him assert very distinctly in German, "Handel is the greatest composer that ever lived." I cannot describe to you with what pathos, and I am inclined to say, with what sublimity of language, he spoke of the *Messiah* of this immortal genius. Every one of us was moved when he said, "I would uncover my head, and kneel down at his tomb!"'

  EDWARD SCHULZ, on a visit to Beethoven; quoted in *The Harmonicon* (January 1824)

'Handel understands effect better than any of us – when he chooses, he strikes like a thunderbolt.'

  WOLFGANG AMADEUS MOZART; quoted in Percy M. Young, *Handel* (1947)

Call Sir Malcolm Sargent old-fashioned, and you'd be right – where 'modern' music, or what he termed 'trivial and banal "tripe"' was concerned. On this subject, he once told his adoring audience at the Last Night of the Proms: 'I wish those of you who have friends who are composers would tell some of them that if they listened a little more to Bach, Beethoven and other classics, read their Shakespeare

and perhaps enjoyed their Bible, they would not
be content to offer us mental obscurities. If I had a
school for composers I would put up two mottoes:
1, if music be the food of love, play on. 2, if not, shut
up, please!'

'I have no aesthetic rules, or philosophy or theories.
I love to write music. I always do it with pleasure,
otherwise I just do not write it.'

DARIUS MILHAUD (1892–1974)

In *Impressions That Remained* (1919), Dame Ethel Smyth
recalls a conversation with Edvard Grieg: 'I ventured to
say that the coda of one of the movements was not quite
up to the level of the rest. "Ah yes!" he said, shrugging
his shoulders, "at that point inspiration gave out and I
had to finish without!"'

'A wonderful genius ... so pleasing and amiable.'

QUEEN VICTORIA, writing in her journal about Mendelssohn
in 1842; quoted in *Chambers Music Quotations* (1991)

'As a musician I tell you that if you were to suppress
adultery, fanaticism, crime, evil, the supernatural, there
would no longer be the means for writing one note.'

GEORGES BIZET; letter (October 1866)

One of the biggest musical upsets of the twentieth century occurred at the Théâtre des Champs-Elysées in Paris on 29 May 1913, when the curtain rose on *Le Sacre du Printemps* ('The Rite of Spring'), an innovative new ballet with choreography by Nijinsky and music by Stravinsky. From the very start, the audience were divided: excited and enthralled, or shocked and angry. Whichever side they were on, this revolutionary work – with its strange dissonances and rhythms, and Nijinsky's sensual dancing – was certainly not what they were accustomed to. And they were quick to make this known to the musicians and dancers.

'First listen! *Then* boo,' the impresario Gabriel Astruc pleaded, as the noise from the audience drowned the orchestra. But to no avail. The shouts, howls, catcalls, hissing and whistling grew in volume, and in some parts of the auditorium developed into fistfights. The police arrived and ejected the worst of the offenders, but pandemonium continued to reign to the very end. As one titled lady complained as she seethed out of the theatre: 'This is the first time in sixty years that anyone has dared to insult me!'

Nor were the critics any more understanding. Most of them loathed the piece even before the curtain went up. One described the score as 'the most dissonant and the most discordant composition yet written'; another critic dubbed the experience, 'Le Massacre du Printemps'.

Critic's Choice

'The music of *Le Sacre du Printemps* ... baffles verbal description. To say that much of it is hideous as sound is a mild description ... Practically it has no relation to music at all as most of us understand the word.'

Musical Times, London (August 1913)

One of Schoenberg's earliest and most successful works was a string sextet, *Verklärte Nacht* ('Transfigured Night'). When many years later he was asked why he no longer composed music like it, he replied: 'I still do, but nobody notices.'

'My music is not modern, it is merely badly played.'
ARNOLD SCHOENBERG; quoted in M. MacDonald,
Schoenberg (1976)

'The modern composer is a madman who persists in manufacturing an article which nobody wants.'
ARTHUR HONEGGER, *I am a Composer* (1951)

'I would rather write 10,000 notes than one letter of the alphabet.'
LUDWIG VAN BEETHOVEN; letter (28 November 1820)

In *Some Musical Recollections of 50 Years* (1910), the Anglo-American pianist and teacher Richard Hoffman (1831–1909) presents a wealth of anecdotes and facts, including this rather novel idea from the Irish composer and singer Michael William Balfe (1808–70) for discovering melodies when inspiration failed: 'He would put the letters of the musical alphabet on separate bits of paper, duplicating each letter several times, then draw them out from a hat, one by one, and note them down, having previously decided upon his key and time. The reiterated notes of some of his melodies certainly warrant the truth of this.'

'Happy tune? Is there such a thing? If so, I never heard it.'
    Attributed to FRANZ SCHUBERT

'How thankful we ought to feel that Wordsworth was only a poet and not a musician. Fancy a symphony by Wordsworth! Fancy having to sit it out! And fancy what it would have been if he had written fugues!'
    SAMUEL BUTLER, *Notebooks* (published 1912)

The title for the most prolific composer of them all probably goes to Georg Philipp Telemann (1681–1767). 'I have always aimed at facility. Music ought not to be an effort,' he said. He also insisted that 'a good composer should be able to set public notices to music'. And though he didn't quite go that far, his output was staggering (more than both J. S. Bach and Handel put together, and they were certainly not slack), including forty operas, two hundred concertos, six hundred French overtures or orchestral suites, and more than a thousand pieces of church music. According to Handel, Telemann 'could write a motet for eight voices more quickly than one could write a letter.' That is fast.

'[Vivaldi] is an old man, who has a prodigious fury for composition. I heard him undertake to compose a concerto, with all the parts, with greater dispatch than a copyist can copy it.'

CHARLES DE BROSSES (1709–77); letter (1739)

What was it about the eighteenth century for writing so fast and so much? Something in the air, in the water, in the ink? Far behind Telemann in the output stakes, but still amazingly prolific, was Antonio Vivaldi (1678–1741). Seven hundred and seventy works, or thereabouts, including 344 solo concertos, 81 for two or more instruments, 61 sinfonias, 46 operas and numerous other vocal and instrumental pieces. Of course, at that rate, it was not always the most original work. As Stravinsky once claimed, Vivaldi wrote not 400 concertos but only one and then copied it out 399 times. Certainly one of the reasons he had to write so much was due to his contract. A priest by vocation (known as *il prete rosso* — 'the red priest' for the colour of his hair), Vivaldi spent much of his career as music master at the Conservatorio dell'Ospedale della Pietà in Venice, a music school for orphaned or illegitimate girls, and his contract stipulated two concertos a month. In 1740 he moved to Vienna, dying there soon afterwards absolutely penniless.

'It is related of him [Vivaldi], that one day, while he was saying Mass, a theme for a fugue having suddenly struck him, he quitted the altar to the surprise of the congregation, hastened into the sacristy to write it down, and, having done so, returned to finish his office. For this misdemeanour he was brought before the Inquisition; but the fault having been considered as an aberration of genius, he received no further punishment than a prohibition from saying Mass for the future.'

GEORGE HOGARTH, *Memoirs of the Musical Drama* (1838)

'When I compose I always feel I am like Beethoven; only afterwards do I become aware that at best I am only Bizet.'

ALBAN BERG (1885–1935); quoted in *Cassell Companion to 20th-century Music* (1997)

The Irish tenor Michael Kelly arrived in Vienna in 1783, became a great friend of Mozart (who refers to Kelly in his own catalogue as 'Occhelly') and created two roles in *The Marriage of Figaro*. In his *Reminiscences* (1826), Kelly gives this sketch of Mozart, who he first met at a concert at a composer's house, where Mozart 'favoured the company by performing fantasias and capriccios on the pianoforte. His feeling, the rapidity of his fingers, the great execution and strength of his left hand, particularly, and the apparent inspiration of his modulations, astounded me. After this splendid performance we sat down to supper, and I had the pleasure to be placed at table between him and his wife, Madame Constance Weber, a German lady of whom he was passionately fond ... After supper the young branches of our host had a dance, and Mozart joined them. Madame Mozart told me that, great as his genius was, he was an enthusiast in dancing, and often said that his taste lay in that art, rather than in music.'

Kelly continues: 'He was a remarkably small man [1.5m, 4ft 11in], very thin and pale, with a profusion of fine fair hair, of which he was rather vain. He gave me a cordial invitation to his house, of which I availed myself, and passed a great part of my time there. He always received me with kindness and hospitality. He was remarkably fond of punch, of which beverage I have seen him take copious draughts. He was also fond of billiards, and had an excellent billiard-table in his house. Many and many a game have I played with him, but always came off second best. He gave Sunday concerts, at which I was never missing. He was kind-hearted, and always ready to oblige, but so very particular when he played, that if the slightest noise were made, he instantly left off.'

'He could conceive wonderful things in music; unfortunately he could not consistently turn them into music.'

NEVILLE CARDUS on Ferruccio Busoni, *Manchester Guardian* (1937)

Critic's Choice

'The Tchaikovsky Fifth Symphony was in part a disappointment ... The second movement showed the eccentric Russian at his best, but the Valse was a farce, a piece of musical padding, commonplace to a degree, while in the last movement, the composer's Calmuck blood got the better of him, and slaughter, dire and bloody, swept across the storm-driven score.'

Musical Courier (13 March 1889)

In 1802 the Irish tenor and composer Michael Kelly proposed to set himself up in the wine trade, and to that end to put up a shop sign reading, 'Michael Kelly, Composer of Music, Importer of Wine'. As there was a suspicion that some of his musical compositions were not entirely his own, his friend, the playwright Richard Brinsley Sheridan (1751–1816) suggested that the sign should read instead: 'Michael Kelly, Composer of Wines and Importer of Music', because 'none of his music is original and all his wine is, since he makes it himself'.

When a young composer asked Hans von Bülow to give an opinion on his latest composition, the distinguished conductor and pianist was dismayed to hear a piece strongly reminiscent of several other composers' works. 'How do you like it?' asked the young composer when he had played it through. Von Bülow replied: 'I have always liked it.'

'Berlioz, musically speaking, is a lunatic; a classical
composer only in Paris, the great city of quacks. His
music is simply and undisguisedly nonsense.'
Dramatic and Musical Review (7 January 1843)

By all accounts, Brahms could be blunt, tactless, rude,
grumpy and, in later life, downright boorish – and
just as much to his friends as to anyone else. After one
gathering in Vienna, where he had been very much on
the offensive, he stormed out of the room – only to
return momentarily to say, 'If there is anyone here I have
not insulted, I beg his pardon.'

Occasionally, Brahms was capable of surprising tact.
The story goes, for instance, that Max Bruch (1838–1920)
arrived one day with the score of his first violin
concerto. Would Brahms be so kind as to look at it and
give his opinion. Brahms read the score from beginning
to end, and – well, he couldn't think of a single good
word to say. Finally, with Bruch standing by expectantly,
he asked: 'Tell me, this manuscript paper ... where *did*
you get it?'

When Classic FM conducted its first Hall of Fame poll
in 1996, in which listeners were invited to name their
top three works of classical music, most people expected
Beethoven or Mozart to come out top. Surprisingly,

however – or perhaps not – the vote for the most popular work went to Bruch's First Violin Concerto. In the 1997 poll, and again in 1998, the number one position remained unchanged.

Tickling the ivories
KEYBOARDS AND KEYBOARDERS

L EST WE FORGET THAT A PIANO IS A STRINGED
INSTRUMENT, we have always ready to hand Leigh
Hunt's reminder that: 'A pianoforte is merely a harp
in a box.' Yes! But what a harp! The piano, surely, of all the
instruments – with the possible exception of other stringed
instruments such as the harp and violin – has the capacity
to move us. Well, not according to my fellow countryman
Oscar Wilde, who once remarked to a friend: 'I assure you
that the typewriting machine, when played with expression,
is not more annoying than the piano when played by a sister
or near relation.' Oh! Come, come, Oscar, what about the
greats!? Well, at least one of the literary greats had the
solution. It was when Edith Sitwell was heard to remark in
a fury: 'I wish the Government would put a tax on pianos
for the incompetent'.

In this section you'll meet masters of the keyboard such
as Schnabel, the Rubinsteins (Anton and Arthur, but no
relation), Horowitz, Paderewski, and 'probably the most
astonishing and successful solo pianist the world had ever
seen', Franz Liszt. Like the notes on the piano, the stories
are black and white: unlike the notes they are all sharp,
with no flats!

𝄞

Piano, *n*. A parlor utensil for subduing the impenitent visitor. It is operated by depressing the keys of the machine and the spirits of the audience.

    AMBROSE BIERCE, *The Devil's Dictionary* (1911)

Mozart once challenged Haydn to play at sight a piece he had composed just that afternoon. Agreeing on a prize of a case of champagne, Haydn accepted the challenge, seated himself at the piano and began to play. Confidently he whisked through the first few bars, and then stopped dead, for the composition suddenly demanded him to play with a hand at either end of the keyboard and at the very same time to strike a note in the centre. Protesting that this was physically impossible, Haydn admitted himself beaten. Mozart took his place at the piano, began again from the beginning and, at the impossible note, bent forward and played it with his nose.

Murphy's Law dictates that if anything can go wrong, it will – even in piano recitals. But rarely has there been such a catalogue of mishaps as that suffered by an aspiring American pianist at Bangkok's Erewan Hotel in July 1972. According to the *Bangkok Post* the pianist was barely into his first piece – Bach's D minor Toccata and Fugue – when, due to the high humidity, the D above middle C began to stick. To make matters worse, he was at the same time experiencing difficulty with a piano stool that had been so overgreased that in one of the toccata's more vigorous sections, he found himself facing the audience. Wisely, he abandoned Bach and turned to Liszt: his Fantasia in G minor. Now the G below middle C began to stick. In an attempt to unstick the note, the pianist gave the lower section of the piano a mighty kick. Its left leg collapsed, and the instrument tilted precariously. At this point, the pianist rose, bowed with dignity, and left the room, only to return moments later with a fire axe to wreak his revenge. Alerted to the noise of splintering piano, the hotel manager intervened with two security guards, who disarmed the hapless musician and dragged him away.

'Liszt is a mere commonplace person, with his hair on end — a snob out of Bedlam. He writes the ugliest music extant.'

   Dramatic and Musical Review (7 January 1843).
[Incidentally, the word 'snob' here is used in the sense of a vulgar, ostentatious person.]

Writing at four o'clock one morning in his *Journal* in Ghent, Belgium, Scottish historian Thomas Carlyle (1795–1881) set down the following heartfelt impression: 'If the Devil some good night should take his hammer and smite in shivers all and every piano of our European world, so that in broad Europe there was not one piano left soundable, would the harm be great? Would not, on

the contrary, the relief be considerable? For once
that you hear any real music from a piano, do
you not five hundred times hear mere artistic
somersaults, distracted jangling, and the hapless pretence
of music?'

'The music teacher came twice each week to bridge the
awful gap between Dorothy and Chopin.'

GEORGE ADE; quoted in *The Frank Muir Book* (1976)

'I am now in pursuit of getting the finest piece of
music that ever was heard; it is a thing that will play
eight tunes,' wrote Horace Walpole in 1737 about
a rather unusual organ. 'Handel and all the great
musicians say, that it is beyond any thing they can
do; and this may be performed by the most ignorant
person; and when you are weary of those eight tunes,
you may have them changed for any other that you
like. This I think much better than going to an Italian
opera, or an assembly. This performance has been
lately put into a Lottery, and all the royal family
chose to have a great many tickets, rather than to
buy it, the price being I think 1000 pounds [around
£75,000 in present-day money], infinitely a less sum
than some bishopricks have been sold for. And
a gentleman won it, who I am in hopes will sell it,
and if he will, I will buy it, for I cannot live to have
another made, and I will carry it into the country
with me.'

> The Abbé Liszt
> Hit the piano with his fist.
> That was the way
> He used to play.

E. C. BENTLEY, *Biography for Beginners* (1905)

The composer Erik Satie frequently provided eccentric instructions for those preparing to play his music. But for heaven's sake, what's a pianist supposed to make of this one: 'To be played with both hands in the pocket'?

Critic's Choice

Reviewing a performance of Bartók's Concerto for Pianoforte and Orchestra at which the composer was the soloist, the *Cincinnati Enquirer* of 26 February 1928 commented: 'Bartók plays the piano part from memory. How does he do it? And would it make any difference if memory failed and different notes were substituted for those written in the score? Perhaps the unaccountable chaos of sound was caused by an incorrect distribution of the parts to the musicians ...'

Among the attributes listed in *Grove's Dictionary* of Ukrainian pianist Vladimir de Pachman is his 'eccentric platform manner'. According to Harold C. Schonberg in *The Great Pianists*, this certainly manifested itself during a Chopin recital in London – a recital attended by his fellow Ukrainian, the pianist Moriz Rosenthal. As he played Chopin's 'Minute' Waltz, Pachman adopted a very odd position, hunching his body over the keyboard as if to hide his hands. Feeling an explanation was in order, he told his audience: 'You know why I do this? I tell you. I do this because in the audience is Moriz Rosenthal, and I do not wish him to copy my fingering!'

Chopin's 'Minute' Waltz, a critic once wrote, 'gives listeners a bad quarter of an hour.'

'The harpsichord, however it may sound in a small room – and to my mind it never has a pleasant sound – in a large concert room sounds just like the ticking of a sewing machine.'

RALPH VAUGHAN WILLIAMS; quoted in *Chambers Music Quotations* (1991)

'Le concert, c'est moi,' said Franz Liszt, and with good reason, since he virtually invented the solo piano recital in 1839. Until that time, concert programmes had been shared by several artists. Liszt also changed for evermore the position of the piano on the platform, having it placed not with the pianist's back to the audience, as was the custom, but sideways on. The great advantage of this for Liszt, of course, was that the ladies could gaze adoringly at his striking profile. Occasionally, he even had two pianos on stage back to back, so that midway through a recital he could change sides and let the audience see his other, equally striking profile. In a way — through the manager of his concert appearances in London — Liszt is also responsible for the word 'recital'. In its musical context, it first appeared in print on an announcement for the Hanover Square Rooms, London, on 9 June 1840: 'M. Liszt will give Recitals on the Pianoforte of the following pieces ...'

'Turn your eyes to any one composition that bears the name of Liszt, if you are unlucky enough to have such a thing on your pianoforte, and answer frankly, if it contains one bar of genuine music. Composition indeed! — decomposition is the proper word for such hateful fungi, which choke up and poison the fertile plains of harmony, threatening the world with drought.'

    Musical World, London (30 June 1855)

Having sat through a harpsichord recital, a music lover described the sound as 'a performance on a bird-cage with a toasting fork'. Typically, Sir Thomas Beecham was more forthright about the instrument: 'Like two skeletons copulating on a corrugated tin roof.'

Mozart once heard a pig squeal. 'G sharp!' he cried. His father went to the piano and played G sharp. The boy was right. At the time he was two years old.

The Polish harpsichordist Wanda Landowska (1879–1959) was hugely influential in modern harpsichord playing and in the instrument's twentieth-century revival. She also held strong views on the way Bach should be interpreted. Confronted one day by a harpsichordist with opposing views she was soon locked in heated discussion. Finally, Landowska extricated herself from the no-win situation: 'Well, my dear,' she said, 'you play Bach *your* way, and I'll continue to play him *his* way.'

Johann Sebastian Bach, on playing the organ: 'There is nothing to it. You only have to hit the right notes at the right time and the instrument plays itself.'

In *My Young Years*, Arthur Rubinstein recalls a bloody experience during a concert in Columbus, Ohio: 'I had just begun to play the first movement of a Beethoven sonata when the nail of my thumb, twisted between two white keys, ripped open. A gush of blood covered the whole keyboard, but I continued to play, ignoring the pain, completely involved in my work. Only when I had finished the movement did the pain become so acute that I had to leave the stage to have the finger bandaged. When I returned to continue the sonata on the freshly cleaned keyboard, my listeners burst into applause. They had been in doubt, when they saw the blood, whether I would be able to finish the concert. The papers, next morning, gave more space to my "Spartan feat" than to my performance.'

'The clavichord gives a fretful waspish kind of sound, not at all suited to tender expression.'

Encyclopaedia Britannica (1801)

In his biography of the French composer Charles Gounod (*Gounod*, 1973), James Harding offers this anecdote concerning a piano recital by Sir Charles Hallé one afternoon in Paris. At a reception later that same day, Gounod approached Hallé and thanked him for the great pleasure his recital had given him, particularly one passage that had affected him deeply. Momentarily, he hummed an extract from a Beethoven sonata, and then continued effusively: 'No one, my dear friend, no one but Hallé could have interpreted that in so masterly a way. Even with my eyes shut, I should have known it was you.' At that point, Madame Gounod approached Hallé and apologised for her husband's absence from the recital that afternoon, due, she explained, to a previous engagement.

In 1919, pianist and patriot Paderewski was appointed Poland's first prime minister. Attending the Paris Peace Conference shortly afterwards, he was introduced to French premier Georges Clemenceau, who asked: 'Are you any relation of that famous pianist Ignaz Jan Paderewski?' 'I *am* that famous pianist,' Paderewski replied. 'And now you are prime minister,' said Clemenceau. 'What a comedown.'

'Piano-playing is more difficult than statesmanship. It is harder to wake emotions in ivory keys than it is in human beings.'

IGNAZ JAN PADEREWSKI

'Never Assume' is the motto in this story about the Italian pianist and composer, Ferruccio Busoni. On a concert tour of Spain around the early years of this century, Busoni arrived one morning in a small town. In those days, pianists such as Busoni sometimes took their own pianos (and occasionally their own tuners) from one venue to the next. After sending his piano ahead to the theatre where he was to give his recital that evening, Busoni enjoyed a leisurely lunch and an even more leisurely afternoon. And that evening he walked on to the stage, bowed to the audience, then turned to find his piano still in its packing case.

In his memoirs *Am I Too Loud?* the accompanist Gerald Moore relates an experience about those unsung heroes of recitals, the pianists' page-turners: 'Slow-coaches provide the less reverent members of the audience with some amusement because they see the accompanist going red in the face, bobbing his head up and down to indicate he wants the page turned, and they hope he is going to have a fit. To one such helper I addressed myself very quietly after one movement of a violin sonata: "If you cannot read the music, why don't you turn the page when I nod my head?" "Because", replied he with some heat, "your head is bobbing up and down all the time."'

In his *Hodgepodge*, J. Bryan III records that in the Solomon Islands, the pidgin English for 'piano' is *bokkis yupala hittim i tok* — 'box-you-hit-him-he-talks'.

Getting up in the morning was a real problem for Anton Rubinstein. Or, rather, not so much a problem for him as for his wife, who frequently had to cancel appointments and make his apologies because he was still in bed. It seemed that nothing could rouse him from his slumber. Finally Madame Rubinstein hit upon a novel idea: she went to the piano and played an incomplete chord. Now to some musicians this is rather like a picture hanging at an angle. As the picture demands to be straightened, so the chord demands to be completed. And so it was for Rubinstein. His sleep disturbed by such dissonance, he leapt out of bed and rushed to the piano to complete the chord. In the interim, his wife rushed into the bedroom and pulled off the bedclothes.

And on the subject of incomplete chords, this anecdote concerns Johann Sebastian Bach. Seeing him enter the room at a gathering one evening, Bach's host — who had been improvising at the keyboard — jumped up from his seat, leaving behind him a dissonant chord. Walking straight past the man, Bach went immediately to the harpsichord, resolved the dissonance and then proceeded with a suitable cadence. Only then did he greet his host.

'With all J. S. Bach's amiable qualities, he had a warm and hasty temper. On one occasion Görner, the organist at St Thomas', who generally played very well, struck a false chord, and Bach flew into such a passion that he tore his wig off, and threw it at the unfortunate man's head, with the thundered exclamation, "You should have been a cobbler rather than an organist!"'

C. H. BITTER, *The Life of Johann Sebastian Bach* (1873)

'Lose no opportunity of practising on the organ; there is no instrument which takes a swifter revenge on anything unclear or sloppy in composition and playing.'

ROBERT SCHUMANN, *Aphorisms* (c. 1833)

The American avant-garde composer George Antheil became so used to shock and anger at his performances that he began carrying a gun whenever he performed. At a concert in Budapest in 1923, his harsh and dissonant music so outraged the audience that they rioted. In spite of this hostile reception, Antheil was determined that his music be heard. At his next concert, he waited until the audience were seated, then ordered the ushers to lock the doors. This done, he approached the piano, and in full view of the audience, slowly took the revolver from its holster and laid it beside him. And there it stayed for the entire performance, as the audience listened attentively to his playing and his music.

At one performance of a Mozart piano concerto, both the soloist and the conductor, Sir Thomas Beecham, gave what may politely be described as 'uninspired' performances. During the intermission, the stage manager went to Beecham and asked, 'Shall we take the piano off the stage or leave it on?' Beecham thought for a moment and then replied, 'You might as well leave it on,' he said. 'It'll probably slink off by itself.'

When it comes to confidence – or nerve – youth knows no bounds. Sitting at the clavier with the emperor, Francis I, beside him, the six-year-old Mozart was about to play a concerto by the music master of the imperial household Georg Christoph Wagenseil (1688–1779), when he decided he needed the composer's presence. 'He ought to be here,' he explained. 'He understands the thing.' Wagenseil was duly sent for. When he arrived, Mozart asked the emperor to relinquish his place at the clavier, then told the elderly composer: 'I am going to play one of your concertos. Will you turn over for me?'

The biggest hands in the keyboard business were probably Sergei Rachmaninov's. With a span of twelve white notes, 28 cm (11 in), his left hand could play a chord of C-E♭-G-C and G, and his right hand a chord of C-E-G-C and E.

Life on the road could be problematic for a pianist on

a recital tour of old India, especially if you had to rely on someone else providing the piano. In his memoirs, Mark Hambourg describes a few unforgettable venues. For instance, there was the town where he had to cancel the concert because – due to an unseasonably cold spell shortly before he arrived – the owner of the one available piano had decided it would be more use as firewood. On another occasion, Hambourg was en route to Peshawar on the North-West Frontier, when he received a telegram asking him to postpone the concert for a week, 'as some light-hearted soldiers had poured a bottle of whisky into the piano, and it would take several days to dry'. But the highlight came in Lahore, where two of the keys stuck in the middle of a sonata. The tuner was sent for. Armed with a pair of pincers he dived into the back of the keys and extracted two enormous cockroaches, who were dining on the felts. His job well done, the triumphant tuner paraded the intruders to loud cheers and applause from a delighted audience.

'Joking apart, Prince Albert asked me to go to him on Saturday at two o'clock so that I may try his organ.'
    FELIX MENDELSSOHN; quoted in Ferruccio Bonavia, *Musicians on Music* (1956)

'It's organ organ organ all the time with him.'
    Mrs Organ Morgan, in Dylan Thomas's *Under Milk Wood* (1954)

'I, too, played the organ frequently in my youth, but my nerves could not withstand the power of this gigantic instrument. I should place an organist who is master of his instrument at the very head of all virtuosi.'

LUDWIG VAN BEETHOVEN; letter to an organist (*c.* 1825)

'Respect the pianoforte! It gives a single man command over something complete: in its ability to go from very soft to very loud in one and the same register it excels all other instruments. The trumpet can blare but not sigh; the flute is contrary; the pianoforte can do both. Its range embraces the highest and lowest practicable notes. Respect the pianoforte!'

FERRUCCIO BUSONI, *Sketch of a New Aesthetic of Music* (1911)

Shortly before joining Sir Thomas Beecham on the concert platform one evening, Dame Myra Hess asked him: 'Are you going to conduct by heart again tonight?' 'Naturally,' Beecham replied. 'In that case,' said Dame Myra, '*I* am going to use my music.'

'There is always a piano in an hotel drawing-room, on which, of course, some one of the forlorn ladies is generally employed. I do not suppose that these pianos are in fact, as a rule, louder and harsher, more violent and less musical, than other instruments of the kind. They seem to be so, but that, I take it, arises from the exceptional mental depression of those who have to listen to them.'

ANTHONY TROLLOPE (1815–82), *North America* (1862)

'I find piano practising a great effort, yet one dare not ignore it. It's like an animal whose heads are continually growing again, however many one cuts off.'

FERRUCCIO BUSONI; letter (1907)

In *The Eighth Octave*, pianist Mark Hambourg recalls a conversation with a well-known player who had changed from playing 'the more sonorous German pianos to the lighter-toned French ones'. When Hambourg asked why, the man replied: 'I found every time I gave a concert on a German instrument the critics wrote next day: "What a fine piano, but what a bad pianist!" Now I play a French one they write: "What a bad piano, but what a fine pianist."'

'There are three kinds of pianists: Jewish pianists, homosexual pianists, and bad pianists.'

VLADIMIR HOROWITZ

During a chaotic rehearsal for Beethoven's Fourth Piano Concerto, soloist Artur Schnabel caught his conductor's attention and asked: 'You are there, I am here — but *where* is Beethoven?'

In his autobiographical *No Minor Chords*, André Previn describes the time he walked on stage to play Stravinsky's Piano Serenade at a concert in Hollywood, only to see the composer himself sitting in the first row. 'It was roughly as though Mount Rushmore had suddenly been placed into the auditorium. I played in a sweat. Applause. I went backstage. The door opened and Stravinsky came over to me. I was very young, and totally devoid of speech. The great man gazed at me, his face expressionless, and then he uttered only one sentence: "You have wonderful fingers." With that, he left, stranding me in an enigmatic fog. Was it a compliment? Was it damning? I didn't know then, and I certainly don't want to know now ...'

'Rubinstein gave seven historical recitals in all the great cities of Europe, usually for the paying public in the evening, and the following morning free for students. Each recital lasted at least two hours. The manager of Bechstein who supplied the pianos for these concerts was asked by a music lover who was interested in the phenomenal programmes what the pianist was playing that evening. "Bechstein, of course," was the unexpected answer.'

MARK HAMBOURG, *The Eighth Octave* (1951)

'The cinema organ, not to be confused with the church organ, shares pride of place for sheer horror with the saxophone, the harmonica and the concertina. They are all incapable of producing other than ignoble sounds.'

GERALD MOORE, *Am I Too Loud?* (1962)

When the full organ joins the tuneful choir,
Th' Immortal Pow'rs incline their ear.

ALEXANDER POPE, *Ode for Musick, on St Cecilia's Day* (*c.*1708)

When the Italian composer and teacher Nicola Porpora (1686–1768) visited a monastery in Germany, the monks invited him to be present at the service, in order that he might hear the organist. Afterwards, the prior asked: 'What do you think of our organist?' 'He is a clever man,' Porpora replied. 'And a good charitable man, too!' interrupted the prior. 'His simplicity is really evangelical.' 'Oh,' said Porpora, 'as to his simplicity, I observed that; for his left hand knoweth not what his right hand doeth.'

'Brahms – what a pianist! One of ten thumbs!'
> PHILIP HALE, music critic of the *Boston Herald*; quoted in
> *The Guinness Dictionary of More Poisonous Quotes* (1992)

Polish-born American pianist Leopold Godowsky (1870–1938) was in the middle of a Chopin recital before a packed house, when fellow pianist Vladimir de Pachman rushed onto the stage. 'No, no, Leopold,' he cried, 'you have to play it like *this*!' And to the audience's delight and Godowsky's fury, he proceeded to play through the entire piece as he thought it should be played. Finally, he turned to the audience, accepted their applause, and explained that he would not have done such a thing for just any player. 'But,' he said, 'Godowsky is the second greatest living pianist!'

'A gentleman knows how to play the accordion, but doesn't.' You can imagine what an accordionist would say if he knew that the man responsible for this now legendary quote, Al Cohn (1925–88), was by profession a saxophonist.

Pride of place in the Beethoven museum in Bonn is the piano on which the composer created some of his masterpieces. Visiting the museum one day, a young American student became so entranced with this piano that she could not bear to leave until she had played just a few bars on it. At first the museum guard refused to let her near it, but in the end a generous tip was offered and accepted. The girl seated herself at the piano and ever so carefully went through the opening of the 'Moonlight' Sonata. After she had finished, she thanked the guard, and said, 'I suppose all the great pianists who come here want to play that piano.' The guard shook his head. 'Not all, Fräulein,' he said. 'Paderewski was here some years ago, and he didn't think himself worthy to touch it.'

When the subject of Grieg came up during a dinner party at Arthur Rubinstein's house, Rachmaninov declared Grieg's Piano Concerto the greatest ever written. By chance, Rubinstein had just finished a new recording of the work, and even had the proofs with him. When he mentioned this fact, Rachmaninov insisted on hearing them. So, after dinner, Rubinstein put on the new recording, and with eyes closed, Rachmaninov sat and listened attentively. After the very last notes had faded away, he opened his eyes and said merely, 'Piano out of tune.'

When he heard that Artur Schnabel had failed his physical for the Austrian army, Moriz Rosenthal quipped: 'What did you expect? No fingers!'

Arthur Rubinstein was standing in the lobby of a concert hall proudly watching the audience filing in to hear one of his recitals. Finally, when the last one had gone in, Rubinstein made a move to enter. An usher blocked his way. 'Sold out, mister,' he said, and to reinforce his words he pointed to a sign beside the box office announcing just that. Rubinstein smiled: 'Sold out. I know,' he said, and made another move. 'You don't understand,' said the usher. 'There ain't no seats left. We can't seat you.' And Rubinstein replied: 'May I be seated at the piano?'

For many years before the First World War, leading piano-makers such as Bechstein, Erard, Blüthner, and Steinway, found it advantageous to provide pianos and sometimes tuners for concert pianists travelling abroad. The instruments were kept in the best condition, the players obtained the piano they preferred and were accustomed to, and the piano-makers benefited not only from the publicity, but also from the sale of the piano after the concert to some delighted member of the public. For Mark Hambourg, however, this arrangement went somewhat awry during a South African tour.

Arriving in Durban for three concerts, he discovered that the piano supplied had already been sold, and though he implored the proud purchaser for the brief use of it, she refused. As far as she was concerned the piano was now her rightful property, and she wasn't about to let it out of her sight – not even to a celebrated concert pianist.

'To play the organ properly one should have a vision of Eternity.'

CHARLES-MARIE WIDOR (1844–1937)

'A man of various moods ... alert, humorous, delightful ... sensational, empty, vulgar and violent ...' is how the music critic George Bernard Shaw once summed up the Polish star pianist Paderewski. Shaw also wrote, somewhat ambiguously: 'Regarded as an immensely spirited young harmonious blacksmith, who puts a concerto on the piano as upon an anvil, and hammers it out with an exuberant enjoyment of the swing and strength of the proceedings.'

When the inventor of the nocturne, John Field (1782–1837), lay dying in a room in Moscow, some friends decided the time had come to send for a clergyman to administer the last rites. However, they were unsure of the Irishman's religious background. 'Are you a Catholic?' they asked him. 'No,' he said. 'A Protestant?' 'No.' 'Then you must be a Calvinist?' they asked. 'No,' he replied. 'I am ... a pianist.'

Invited to write an opera for the King's Theatre in London, Rossini travelled to England in December 1823. The king, George IV, received him warmly, and invited him to be his accompanist as he sang. Unfortunately, the king wandered into a different key, and Rossini continued to play as though nothing had happened. When questioned about this afterwards, Rossini explained tactfully: 'It was my duty to accompany your Majesty. I am ready to follow you wherever you may go.'

At one of Schnabel's recitals, an elderly lady in the front row fell asleep at the start and only awoke at the end as the audience enthusiastically demonstrated their approval. Seeing the lady startled from her slumber, Schnabel leaned over to her. 'It was the applause, madame,' he told her gently. 'I played as softly as I could.'

Following a Paderewski recital at London's St James's Hall in 1890, the critic of the *Daily Telegraph* wrote: 'We do not like Mr Paderewski. The result of his labours may be marvellous, but it is not music.'

One of the criticisms levelled at Paderewski was his inaccuracy, but as Harold C. Schonberg notes in *The Great Pianists*: 'While his competitors were counting his wrong notes, he was counting his dollars.' Paderewski is reputed to have been the highest paid classical concert pianist ever.

At the première of the C minor Concerto, Beethoven asked his friend, the Austrian composer and conductor Ignaz Ritter von Seyfried (1776–1841), to turn the pages for him, but – as he describes it – that was easier said than done. 'I saw almost nothing but empty leaves; at the most on one page or the other a few Egyptian hieroglyphs wholly unintelligible to me scribbled down to serve as clues for him; for he played nearly all of the solo part from memory, since, as was so often the case, he had not had time to put it all on paper. He gave me a secret glance whenever he was at the end of one of the invisible passages and my scarcely concealable anxiety not to miss the decisive moment amused him greatly and he laughed heartily at the jovial supper which we ate afterwards.'

'The Winchester Cathedral organ is audible at five miles, painful at three and lethal at one.'

ANON; quoted in *The Guinness Dictionary of More Poisonous Quotes* (1992)

'With the advent of electronic organs – the wonderful old paaah and chaah became just plain aaah.'

E. P. BIGGS, *Newsweek* (1977)

The Erard brothers, founders of a well-respected Parisian firm of piano and harp makers in the 1780s, made a number of customised pianos. Among these was a portable one for Napoleon to take on his campaigns.

It had a special pedal which, when depressed, struck a drum — for the odd martial nocturne, no doubt.

When it came to playing the piano, Wagner was certainly nothing to write home about, and he knew it. But if anyone ever commented on this, he replied: 'I play a good deal better than Berlioz.' In fact, there was no contest there: Berlioz couldn't play at all.

After Paderewski played at a royal command performance at Windsor, Queen Victoria exclaimed with delighted enthusiasm, 'Mr. Paderewski, you are a genius!' Always very proud of his diligence in practising, the 'genius' replied: 'Perhaps, Your Majesty, but before I was that, I was a drudge.'

'The notes I handle no better than many pianists. But the pauses between the notes — ah, that is where the art resides.'

Artur Schnabel; quoted in *Chicago Daily News* (11 June 1958)

When Anton Rubinstein was practising, his servant, François, made sure that no one disturbed him. On one occasion, a lady telephoned wishing to speak to Rubinstein. Although the piano was clearly audible in the background, François assured the lady that his master was not at home. 'But,' she insisted, 'he is playing. I hear him.' 'Madame, you are mistaken,' replied the servant. 'It is I, dusting the piano keys.'

J. B. Morton's definition of a prodigy: 'A child who plays the piano when he ought to be asleep in bed.'

In *The Unimportance of Being Oscar*, Oscar Levant recalls a concert in which the Canadian Glenn Gould played the Brahms D Minor Concerto. 'Gould gave a very languid interpretation to this pretentious work ... his rendition established a world's record. It lasted fifteen minutes longer than any previous playing. Afterward Irving Kolodin, the music editor of the *Saturday Review*, asked Gould why he had done it that way. He replied: "I felt very baroque".'

'There is nothing that soothes me more after a long and maddening course of piano-forte recitals than to sit and have my teeth drilled by a finely skilled hand,' said George Bernard Shaw, when a musical critic.

'I used to be an organist.' 'Really? Why did you give it up?' 'The monkey died.'

Although Paderewski was for many years the darling of the concert-going public, fellow pianists did not rate him highly. Following one of Paderewski's recitals, Moriz Rosenthal is reported to have commented, 'He plays well, I suppose, but he's no Paderewski.' Many years later, Rosenthal accompanied a colleague to one of Paderewski's several farewell performances. By this time it was clearly evident from his playing that the old man was no longer at his best. 'Ah, the things he has forgotten!' murmured Rosenthal's colleague. To which Rosenthal retorted: 'What he forgets is not so bad. It's what he *remembers!*'

'The upright piano is a musical growth found adhering to the walls of most semi-detached houses in the provinces.'

SIR THOMAS BEECHAM

In 1828, a certain Mr Scarborough, the organist of Spalding in Lincolnshire, accepted a bet that he would strike one million notes on the piano in the space of twelve hours. This 'singular wager' was decided on the 4th of June of that year. According to Hone's *Year Book* (1838), Spalding took a spread of three octaves, and, ascending and descending the different scales, proceeded to strike as follows: 109,296 notes in the first hour, 125,928 in the second, 121,176 in the third, 121,176 in the fourth, 125,136 in the fifth, 125,136 in the sixth, 127, 512 in the seventh, 127,512 in the eighth, and 47,520 in twenty minutes. In this way, he managed in eight hours and twenty minutes to strike 1,030,392 notes, which, together with the 'periods of rest', amounted to eleven hours and forty-five minutes.

[To appreciate fully the following tale from Charles Villiers Stanford's *Pages from an Unwritten Diary*, it may help to know that in 1865 the virtuoso pianist and conductor Franz Liszt received minor orders in the Catholic Church, and was therefore known as 'Abbé'.]
'A young lady pianist had announced a recital, advertising herself (in the hope of attracting a larger audience) as a "pupil of Liszt". As she had never laid eyes on him in her life, she was horrified to read in the papers on the morning of her concert that the Abbé had arrived in the city. The only thing to be done was to make a clean breast of it; she went to his hotel and asked for an interview. When she was shown in she confessed with many tears, and asked for absolution. Liszt asked her the name of the pieces she was going to play, chose one and made her sit down at the piano and play it. Then he gave her some hints about her performance, and dismissed her with a pat on the cheek, and the remark, "Now, my dear, you can call yourself a pupil of Liszt".'

'Bach is the foundation of piano playing, Liszt the summit. The two make Beethoven possible.'
    FERRUCCIO BUSONI; letter (1898)

During a train journey to a concert rehearsal, Josef Hofmann sat motionless, his eyes glazed, his brow furrowed in deep concentration. For about fifteen minutes or so, a passenger sitting opposite stared in fascination. Eventually the man could contain his curiosity no more. 'Excuse me for asking,' he asked Hofmann, 'but what are you doing?' The pianist looked at him disdainfully and replied: 'I *was* practising.'

Peter Philips (?1561–1628), the second most published English composer of his day, relates this incident about his even more successful contemporary John Bull (?1562–1628) and a surprise encounter with Queen Elizabeth, who was at the time 'at the virginalls' [a small, legless rectangular harpsichord; so-called because it was usually played by young girls]: 'Maister Bull did come by stealthe to heare without, and by mischaunce did sprawle intoe the queenes Maiesties Presence, to the queenes great disturbance. Shee demaundinge incontinent the wherefore of suche presumption, Maister Bull with great skill sayd that wheresoever Maiesty and Musicke so well combyned, no man mighte abase himself too deeplie; whereupon the queenes Maiesty was mollifyde and sayd that so rayre a Bull hath song as sweete as Byrd.'

Quoted in *Chambers Music Quotations* (1991)

Late in his long life, Arthur Rubinstein continued to perform regularly in public, and to make records, including the entire works of Chopin. This led him once to remark: 'Sometimes I think, not so much am I a pianist, but a vampire. All my life I have lived off the blood of Chopin.'

'The sonatas of Mozart are unique; they are too easy for children and too difficult for artists.'

ARTUR SCHNABEL, *My Life and Music*; quoted in Nat Shapiro, *Encyclopedia of Quotations about Music* (1978)

A child prodigy was sent to Moriz Rosenthal for assessment. 'How old are you?' he asked. 'Seven,' said the child. 'And what are you going to play for me?' 'The Tchaikovsky Concerto.' 'Too old!' cried Rosenthal.

During his early days in Hollywood in the 1950s, André Previn regularly performed a variety of piano compositions in a 'prestigious series' known as the Monday Evening Concerts. One occasion was particularly memorable. It began when the director of the concert series telephoned him to ask if he could stand in as the other pianist in a forthcoming performance of Mozart's Two-Piano Sonata in D. Previn was flattered by the invitation but declined: it was a difficult piece, he had never played it before, and as the concert was only a few days away there wouldn't be time enough to rehearse. The director assured him there wouldn't be a problem, as his fellow pianist, Lukas Foss, had played the piece many times and would easily guide him through it. Hearing this, Previn accepted. He rang Foss and arranged to play through the sonata at his house. When, shortly afterwards, Previn and Foss sat down at the two pianos, Previn felt an apology was in order: 'I don't know this piece. Never played it before. Thank goodness you're an old hand at it, I need help.' At this, Foss jumped up. '*You've* never played it?' he screamed. '*I've* never played it, but they told me you knew all about it!' As Previn describes it in his autobiography *No Minor Chords*, 'there was a minute's silence while we digested the fact that we had fallen for one of the oldest con games of the entrepreneurial world, and then we both began to laugh. "What the hell," Lukas said, "we've got two whole days, all the time in the world, let's start."'

In his telling of this, Previn adds the following philosophical postscript about the review that appeared in the *Los Angeles Times* the morning after the concert, 'in which it was noted that it had been a pleasure for the critic to hear a performance so carefully studied and prepared and thought-out. Well, it only proves a maxim I have tried hard to remember: It is perfectly correct to disregard all the bad reviews one gets, but only if at the same time, one disregards the good ones as well.'

In her *Memories and Adventures* (1913), the contralto Louise Héritte-Viardot (1841–1918) recalls a critical incident with the composer Rossini, who asked her one day: 'Do you know what Wagner's music sounds like?' Then opening the piano, he seated himself heavily on the keys and exclaimed, 'There! That's the music of the future.'

Accord, *n.* Harmony.
Accordion, *n.* An instrument in harmony with the sentiments of an assassin.

AMBROSE BIERCE, *The Devil's Dictionary* (1911)

'Poor accompanists are admittedly numerous enough, but there are very few good ones, for today everyone wants to be the soloist.'

LEOPOLD MOZART (1756)

In his book *The Well-tempered Accompanist* (1949), Dutch pianist Coenraad van Bos writes of the early days in his career when he accompanied the singer Raymond von zur Mühlen, and how, after their first four concerts together, von zur Mühlen offered only criticism rather than the praise or encouragement Bos had been expecting. The accompanist finally understood after their fifth concert together, when the singer told him: 'You must have played well today for I did not notice you.'

Beethoven once heard a friend's daughter practising his 'Variations on an original theme'. After he had listened for a while he asked her, 'By whom is that?' 'By you,' replied the girl. 'Such nonsense by me! Oh, Beethoven! What an ass you were!'

In October 1705, the 20-year-old Johann Sebastian Bach was given a month's leave from his post as church organist at Arnstadt to travel to Lübeck to hear the celebrated organist of the Marienkirche, Dietrich Buxtehude. Short of money, Bach walked to Lübeck, a distance of roughly 350 km (220 miles). Arriving there many days later, he learned that Buxtehude was about to retire. Bach was offered the lucrative post. But there was one condition: he had to marry Buxtehude's 30-year-old daughter, Anna. Bach declined the offer, but stayed to learn from the master. In January, Bach returned home by foot once more to Arnstadt, where he received an official reprimand from the town's burghers not only for his unofficial absence of three months, but also for the musical changes he now began to make in the usually staid chorales. Incidentally, poor old Buxtehude was not having much luck with marrying off his daughter. Two years before Bach turned up, two other organists, Johann Mattheson and an 18-year-old Georg Friederich Händel, had both been offered the same deal, and refused. For Handel to have succumbed to marriage and a steady job near Hamburg and the newer world of opera might not have changed what eventually happened, but had Bach accepted – how different the course of musical history might have been.

'Rachmaninov was the only pianist I have ever seen who did not grimace. That is a great deal.'

IGOR STRAVINSKY; quoted in Robert Craft, *Conversations with Igor Stravinsky* (1958)

Paderewski once explained the importance of practice: 'If I don't practise for one day, I know it; if I don't for two days, the critics know it; and if I don't for three days, the audience knows it.'

According to this description by contemporary composer André Messager (quoted in Gervase Hughes, *Sidelights on a Century of Music*, 1969), French composer and pianist

Emmanuel Chabrier (1841–94) had a rather unorthodox playing style: 'He would attack the piano not only with his hands but also with his elbows, his forehead, his stomach and even his feet, thereby producing the most unusual effects and a volume of sound akin to that of a ferocious storm; he would only relax when the unfortunate instrument was itself reeling on its legs like a drunken man.'

'One Sunday, having attended divine worship at a country church, Handel asked the organist to permit him to play the people out; to which he readily consented. Handel, accordingly, sat down to the organ, and began to play in such a masterly manner, as instantly to attract the attention of the whole congregation, who, instead of vacating their seats as usual, remained for a considerable space of time, fixed in silent admiration. The organist began to be impatient ... and, at length, addressed the great performer, telling him, he was convinced that *he* could not play the people out, and advised him to relinquish the attempt; for while he played, they would never quit the church.'

THOMAS BUSBY, *Concert Room and Orchestra Anecdotes of Music and Musicians* (1828)

Sir Thomas Beecham was not particularly fond of the organ: 'A mechanical box of whistles', he called it once. In this, he echoed Sir Christopher Wren's feelings about the organ in St Paul's Cathedral: 'a confounded box of whistles'.

In his *Musical Laughs* (1924), Henry Finck recalls a pianist who, much to the annoyance of Moriz Rosenthal, insisted on playing Liszt's Sixth Hungarian Rhapsody at a ridiculously slow tempo. Meeting the pianist in the street one morning, Rosenthal invited the man to pay him a visit. The invitation was declined. 'I would like to so much,' said the man, 'but, alas, I do not have the time.' 'Nonsense!' Rosenthal replied. 'If you have time to play the Liszt's rhapsody like that, you certainly have time to visit me!'

When asked the secret of his success, virtuoso pianist Artur Schnabel replied: 'I always make sure that the lid over the keyboard is open before I start to play.'

'I don't play accurately — anyone can play accurately — but I play with wonderful expression. As far as the piano is concerned, sentiment is my forte. I keep science for life.'

> Algernon in Oscar Wilde's *The Importance of Being Earnest* (1895)

On New Year's Eve 1906, during a particularly rough Atlantic crossing to his début in the United States, pianist Arthur Rubinstein gave a recital in the lounge to take, as he describes it in *My Young Years*, 'passengers' minds off the heaving sea'. He had not been playing long, when an unusual situation developed. 'At one moment, a sudden jerk of the boat made me lose my balance and I fell to the floor, although I was not hurt. When I scrambled to my feet again, the captain gave orders to two sailors to attach my legs with leather straps to the stool, which was secured by hooks to the floor; so was the piano. I continued my concert without further incident, and enjoyed the fact of being "chained to my art".'

'Anton Rubinstein, who may be considered Liszt's successor, played with great volume of tone and swept his hearers off their feet with his power and intensity. He was, notwithstanding this, a very inaccurate performer, owing probably to his spiritual excitement, and his critics said that one could make another sonata with the amount of wrong notes he performed in Beethoven's *Appassionata*. "That may be," said his ardent admirers, "but we should enjoy hearing the second sonata just as much as the original if played by him!"'

MARK HAMBOURG, *The Eighth Octave* (1951)

'I know nothing more beautiful than the *Appassionata*, I could listen to it every day. It is marvellous, unearthly music. Every time I hear these notes, I think with pride and perhaps childlike naïveté, that it is wonderful what man can accomplish. But I cannot listen to music often, it affects my nerves. I want to say amiable stupidities and stroke the heads of the people who can create such beauty in a filthy hell.'

LENIN (1870–1924); quoted by Maxim Gorky, *Days with Lenin* (1933)

'In my eyes and ears the organ will ever be the King of instruments.'

WOLFGANG AMADEUS MOZART; letter (1777)

Dryfat: The organs of the body, as some term them.
Mrs Purge: Organs! fie, fie, they have a most abominable sound in mine ears; they edify not a whit, I detest 'em. I hope my body has no organs.

THOMAS MIDDLETON (*c.* 1570–1627), *The Family of Love* (1608) Act III sc.2

'When music is given at afternoon "at homes", it is usual to listen to the performance, or at least to appear to do so; and if conversation is carried on, it should be done in a low tone, so as not to disturb or annoy the performers.'

'A Member of the Aristocracy', *Manners and Rules of Good Society* (14th edition, 1887)

Glancing at the audience during a recital, Mark Hambourg noticed in the front row of the audience a man reading a newspaper. Hambourg stopped and glared at the man. Becoming aware of the silence, the man looked up from his paper and said: 'Do go on playing, you do not disturb me in the least.'

Franz Liszt once played a command performance for the Emperor of Austria at the Palace of Schönbrun in

Vienna. From the moment he began, he was aware of the emperor's animated conversation with several of his guests. For a while the pianist suffered the disturbance, but at last his patience ran out and he stopped playing, and sat motionless. Now the emperor noticed him. 'Herr Liszt,' he said, 'please continue to play, for you do not inconvenience me at all.' 'Indeed, Sire?' replied Liszt boldly. 'I am sorry, for you inconvenience me greatly.'

Another anecdote concerning inattentive listeners casts Napoleon III in the villain's role. Invited to play for the emperor, Hans von Bülow was very much irritated to hear him chattering to a guest. Finally, von Bülow stopped playing. Eventually, Napoleon noticed the absence of piano music and sent a messenger to ask the player why he was not playing. The player sent back the following message: 'When his majesty speaks, all must be silent.' There was no further interruption. Incidentally, a similar story is also told about Liszt's playing for Czar Nicholas I in St Petersburg. On this occasion, when asked why he had stopped playing, Liszt replied: 'When Nicholas speaks, music herself should be silent.'

If talkers are a nuisance for performers and audience, latecomers are almost as bad. In *The Unimportance of Being Oscar*, pianist Oscar Levant describes his merciless treatment of one culprit as she tottered down the aisle to her seat some time after his recital had begun: 'I stopped my performance of a Poulenc piece and began choreographing her walk by playing in time with her steps. She hesitated and slowed down – I slowed down. She stopped – I stopped. She hurried – I hurried. By the time she reached her seat, the audience was in hysterics and the matron in a state of wild confusion.'

Perhaps Levant received his inspiration for the torture from this similar tale about Hans von Bülow, which was told by John Francis Barnett in *Musical Reminiscences and Impressions* (1906). 'It so happened that two ladies were making their way to their seats at the very moment he finished the introduction of the first movement of Beethoven's Sonata *Pathétique*. This so irritated him that he purposely commenced the allegro at such an absurdly slow pace as to make the quavers in the bass correspond exactly to the time of the ladies' footsteps. As may be imagined, they felt on thorns whilst walking to their places, and hurried on as fast as they possibly could, whilst von Bülow accelerated his tempo in sympathy with their increasing pace. It was only when they had seated themselves that he took the proper speed of the allegro.'

While travelling incognito through Germany, Paderewski stopped for the night at a small country inn. In the main room stood an old battered piano, and, true to form, Paderewski could not resist flexing his fingers. To his dismay, he soon discovered that not only was the instrument badly out of tune, but that some of the keys were stuck and would make no sound at all. When he complained about this, the landlord, somewhat offended by the criticism of his piano, replied, 'You don't know much about about piano playing, do you? Because if you did, you'd skip over those keys so it wouldn't matter.'

Critic's Choice

'If the reader were so rash as to purchase any of Bartók's compositions, he would find that they each consist of unmeaning bunches of notes, apparently representing the composer promenading the keyboard in his boots. Some can be played better with the elbows, others with the flat of the hand. None require fingers to perform, nor ears to listen to.'

FREDERICK CORDER, *Musical Quarterly* (1915)

A would-be concert pianist visited Anton Rubinstein to ask for his opinion of her talent. He invited her to play, and listened patiently as she went through her pieces. 'Well?' she asked when she had finished. 'What do you think I should do now?' 'Get married,' Rubinstein replied.

Following an inspired performance at Carnegie Hall, a critic asked Rachmaninov what sublime thoughts had been passing through his head as he seated himself at the piano to begin. Rachmaninov answered candidly: 'I was counting the house.'

In addition to the task of accompanist to the royal

chamber music, C.P.E. Bach's position as court musician to Frederick the Great also included the task of accompanying the king's flute solos on the piano. This was sometimes a difficult task, since the king, a keen flautist, believed himself much better than he was and often took liberties with the tempo. At the end of one royal performance a delighted sycophant exclaimed: 'Your Majesty, what rhythm!' *'What rhythms!'* Bach muttered under his breath.

'Even an ordinary broken chord is made to disclose rare beauties; we are reminded of the fairies' hazelnuts in which diamonds were concealed but you could break the shell only if your hands were blessed.'

NEVILLE CARDUS, on Rachmaninov's playing, *Manchester Guardian* (1939)

'The whole world is open to me, and success awaits me everywhere. Only one place is closed to me, and that is my own country – Russia.'

RACHMANINOV; quoted in *The Musical Times* (June 1930)

In *The Great Pianists*, Harold C. Schonberg tells the following tale about the Czech pianist Alexander Dreyschock (1818–69) in Vienna: 'At Dreyschock's first court appearance he played before the emperor [Franz Josef] in a very hot room, with closed windows. Dreyschock began to perspire. The emperor listened intently and watched him more closely. When the pianist got up and faced the emperor, he was afraid to wipe his face. The emperor approached. "My dear Dreyschock, I have heard Moscheles play." Dreyschock bowed. "I have heard Thalberg." Dreyschock bowed lower. "I have heard Liszt." Dreyschock bowed very low indeed. "I have heard all the great players. But I never, never, never saw anybody perspire as you do."'

Eager to help a young violinist making his début at Carnegie Hall, the Romanian violinist Georges Enescu (1881–1955) offered to accompany him on the piano. Hearing of the offer, the concert pianist Walter Gieseking (1895–1956) insisted on joining him to turn the pages. The following morning, a review of the performance read: 'The man who should have been playing the piano was turning the pages, and the man who should have been turning the pages was playing the violin.'

An item in *The New Yorker* some fifty years ago relates the occasion when the Australian composer and pianist Percy Grainger (1882–1961), then resident in New York, travelled to suburban Long Island to play for a ladies' club matinée. Meeting Grainger a few days after the event, a friend, who had been at the recital, accused him of giving the ladies an abridged version of Grieg's 'Ballade'. 'That's right,' replied Grainger, 'I dropped six pages out of the middle so I could catch the 4:58.'

On the several occasions that Arthur Rubinstein appeared in a trio with violinist Jascha Heifetz and cellist Gregor Piatigorsky, he insisted on, and was given, top billing. Eventually Heifetz complained: 'If the Almighty himself played the violin, the credits would still read "Rubinstein, God and Piatigorsky".'

Quite apart from his pianistic talents, Josef Hofmann (1876–1957) was noted both for the size of his hands – which were so small that he needed a special keyboard – and his height, or lack of it. When a very tall musician visited Hofmann backstage to congratulate him after a concert, he bent over and declared: 'You are a giant.'

The Ukrainian pianist Vladimir Horowitz emigrated to the United States in the late 1920s. Even so, he never completely mastered English. Greeting Mrs Hoover, wife of the then president, Herbert Hoover, he bowed and said, 'I am delightful.'

Artur Schnabel once offered the young pianist Vladimir Horowitz the following advice: 'When a piece gets difficult, make faces.'

Reviewing Horowitz in the *Manchester Guardian* in 1936, Neville Cardus wrote: 'He is so rare an aromatist of the piano ... that to hear him with an orchestra is like trying to get the best out of champagne while eating roast beef.'

Polish pianist and teacher, Theodor Leschetizky (1830–1915), whose pupils included Paderewski and Schnabel, believed that to be a first-class pianist required three essential ingredients, and part of his audition of a prospective pupil included the following questions: 'Were you a child prodigy?', 'Are you of Slavic descent?', and 'Are you Jewish?' Only if the answer to all three was in the affirmative, would he deign to tutor the young player.

Oscar Levant was in the middle of a recital when the sound of his music was interrupted by a telephone ringing off-stage. The pianist continued playing, the ringing persisted, no one answered, and the audience became distracted. Finally, without a flicker of a pause in his performance Levant turned to his audience and said, 'If that's for me, tell them I'm busy.'

Tongs and bones
ORCHESTRAS AND INSTRUMENTS

S O MANY OF THE STORIES about the instruments of the orchestra seem to centre around the viola (and to a lesser extent the percussionists' section) that it's a temptation to believe that's where it begins and ends. Not so. Orchestras are unique in the performing arts world, simply because no other group of public artists is ever so big: there always seem to be dozens of them! (Have you ever been to the Last Night of the Proms?! Ye Gods!) It was Plato who remarked, unusually you might think coming from him, that music and rhythm find their way into the secret places of the soul. As it's accepted that without the composer we'd have nothing to play, you have to agree equally that without the men, women and children who play, we the listeners would have nothing to listen to. They are good souls, by and large, these orchestras, and taken individually they'll make great companions on a desert island. Collectively they can be a Bolshoi lot as they'd be the first to admit ... try working out who owes what on the restaurant bill after you've had lunch with seven musicians and you'll know what I mean! Where would we be without them and their instruments? As we enter this section, spare a thought for the double bass player trying to get to work on the bus, the man carrying a celeste through airport customs who tries to explain what it does, and even the girl who took her harp to the party and nobody asked her to play!

𝄞

'I have a reasonable good ear in music: let us have the tongs and the bones.'

WILLIAM SHAKESPEARE, *A Midsummer Night's Dream* (1596)

In *Letters to his Wife* (translated by Rosamond Ley, 1938), the composer and pianist Ferruccio Busoni made the following comment about the orchestra: 'Have you ever thought about the "Orchestra"? Each of its members is a poor disappointed devil. Collectively they are like a suppressed crowd of rebels, and, as an official "body", they are bumptious and vain. Routine gives their playing the varnish of perfection and assurance. For the rest, they loathe their work, their job and, most of all, music.'

'The pleasure of conducting does not lie in the actual performance but in the preparation of the performance – the pulling together of the whole thing. This is the conductor's view of the situation: the player's opinion is the opposite. It is a peculiarity of choruses and instrumentalists that they don't like rehearsal.'

SIR HENRY WOOD; quoted in Ates Orga, *The Proms* (1974)

Wagner did not like the saxophone. 'It sounds, like the word

"Reckankreuzungsklankewerkzeuge".'

[This word, by the way, a convoluted collection of puns and allusions, is almost impossible to translate – so we haven't.]

Critic's Choice

'The orchestra is a noble instrument, but it has seldom been put to so ignoble a use as it is in [Prokofiev's] *The Love for Three Oranges.*'

RICHARD ALDRICH, *New York Times* (15 February 1922)

In his musical potpourri, *Off-beat*, Dudley Moore tells of a salutary experience he once had with a horn player: 'There was one particular passage in the piece I'd written that I wanted him to bring out. When he played it though, I thought he was a little out of tune and suggested, as tactfully as I could, "I hate to say it, but you're sounding a little sharp to me." He noted this and we had another go, but that still wasn't right. "I hate to say this," I ventured, "but it's sounding a little flat now." "Listen," he replied, "I can pull in, pull out, or push off!"'

'He was a fiddler, and consequently a rogue.'

JONATHAN SWIFT; letter (25 July 1711)

'One day the principal bassoon did not turn up at rehearsal. Sargent asked the second bassoon (Liverpudlian), if he would be so good as to take over. In a broad Lancashire accent the second bassoon said all right, he'd have a go; but he didn't want "any black looks nor any bloody messing about, neither". By "messing about" he meant being pulled up and told to play something in a different way. The main work in hand that morning was *The Planets*. During the bassoon solo in the *Saturn* section, which is subtitled "The Bringer of Old Age", Sargent rapped the rail and asked Mr X if he couldn't take the phrase in one breath instead of two. "But," objected X, "this tune's supposed to be about an old man, and I'm making it sound like one!" Sargent and every player on the platform except X, who permitted himself a tolerant smile, laughed for minutes over this.'

CHARLES REID, *Malcolm Sargent* (1968)

The world's largest brass instrument is a contrabass tuba, which was constructed *c.*1896–98 for a world tour by the band of the American composer John Philip Sousa (1854–1932). The tuba, with a bell 1m (3ft 3in) across and 11.8m (39ft) of tubing, stands 2.28m (7ft 6in) high.

'Musical people are so absurdly unreasonable. They always want one to be perfectly dumb at the very moment when one is longing to be absolutely deaf.'

OSCAR WILDE, *An Ideal Husband* (1895) Act II

Jew's harp, *n*. An unmusical instrument, played by holding it fast with the teeth and trying to brush it away with the finger.

AMBROSE BIERCE, *The Devil's Dictionary* (1911)

During a rehearsal a violinist's bow brushed the string next to the one he had intended to play. The sound it made was almost inaudible, and hardly anyone could have heard it. Unfortunately for the violinist, the conductor was Toscanini who never missed anything. He immediately stopped the orchestra, directed his baton at the offending player, and cried out: 'One string will be quite enough, if you please.' [Incidentally, as well as his hearing, Toscanini's sight was also to be feared: it's said that he could spot an incorrect bow movement at thirty paces!]

'Give the piper a penny to play, and twopence to leave off.'

THOMAS FULLER, *Gnomologia* (1732)

Having just joined the orchestra, the young percussionist was naturally rather nervous, especially when he discovered that the first item on the rehearsal programme with Sir Thomas Beecham that morning included an important drum solo. As he had never rehearsed with the legendary conductor, the percussionist thought it wise to ask another player how he might like it performed. The player, a hornist, replied: 'Whatever you do, don't hold back. His

hearing's not as good as it was, so make sure it's loud.'
The percussionist thanked the hornist for his advice,
and studied his part. Eventually, Beecham arrived.
'We will begin with the drum solo,' he announced.
Remembering the hornist's advice, the percussionist
vigorously attacked his solo, giving it all he could and
quite a lot extra. Beecham stopped conducting, and
watched coolly. Then when it was all over and the last
vibration had faded away, he said: 'Young man, you
are not a percussionist – you are an anarchist!'

'What do you need to know to play the cymbals?'
someone once asked Sir Malcolm Sargent. 'Nothing,'
he replied. 'Just when.'

Apropos of cymbals, the clarinettist Jack Brymer recalls
in his autobiography *From Where I Sit* (1979) a 'terrible
moment' when the conductor Muir Mathieson (1911–75)
asked 'one of the percussion players to "give that thing
a good bang three bars before C". It was a cymbal, I
think, and Jimmy didn't like being insulted. "Mister
Mathieson," he said. "It isn't a thingg – it's a cymball;
and he dusn't bangg it – he *draws* the *toan* out of it!"'

'What would you have been if you hadn't been a
musician?' 'A drummer!'

One of the least complimentary names for an
orchestra's percussion section (or 'kitchen department'
as it is sometimes known) is 'Bang Gang'.

In defence of percussionists, an item in the May 1897 issue of *The Violin Times* recounts this tale about the English violinist, conductor and critic John Ella (1802–88) when he attended one of Paganini's rehearsals: ' ... the drummer got so alarmed in the presence of the virtuoso that he trembled almost too much to hold his drumsticks; and Ella, laying down his violin, went to the drums and took his place, receiving the thanks of Paganini, who was fast losing his patience with the nervous drummer. Still, drummers who have been abused are not always to blame. We have all heard of the ignorant manager-proprietor who, being present at an orchestra rehearsal, observed that the drummer did next to nothing, and went up to him to expostulate. "But sir," says the drummer, "I'm resting – don't you see?" and he pointed to his part. "Damme, sir," says the manager, "I do not pay you to rest; I pay you to play".'

Critic's Choice

'The drums, the triangles, the cymbals, the tamtams, the eighteen anvils in the *Rhinegold* certainly justify a passing fear that music threatens to end as it began – in noise.'

MAJOR H. W. L. HIME, *Wagnerism, a Protest*; London (1884); quoted in Nicolas Slonismky, *Lexicon of Musical Invective* (1965)

'Handel used to say, "When I came hither first, I found, among the English, many good players and no composers; but now, they are all composers and no players."'

CHARLES BURNEY (1726–1814), *Account of the Musical Performances in Commemoration of Handel* (1785)

'Handel, as is well known, had such a remarkable irritability of nerves, that he could not bear to hear the tuning of instruments, and, therefore, this was always done before he arrived at the theatre. A musical wag, determined to extract some mirth from his irascibility of temper, stole into the orchestra, one night when the Prince of Wales was to be present, and untuned all the instruments. As soon as the Prince arrived, Handel gave the signal to begin, *con spirito*; but such was the horrible discord, that the enraged musician started up from his seat, and, having overturned a double-bass which stood in his way, he seized a kettle-drum, which he threw with such violence at the leader of the band, that he lost his full-bottomed wig in the effort. Without waiting to replace it, he advanced bare-headed to the front of the orchestra, breathing vengeance, but so much choked with passion that utterance was denied him. In this ridiculous attitude he stood staring and stamping for some moments, amidst the general convulsion of laughter; nor could he be prevailed upon to resume his seat, until the Prince went in person, and with much difficulty appeased his wrath.'

THOMAS BUSBY (1755–1838), *Concert Room and Orchestra Anecdotes of Music and Musicians* (1825)

The unsung hero in any concert orchestra is the oboe, which customarily gives the 'A' to which all the other players tune their instruments. That is, of course, if they can. On one rehearsal occasion, hearing that the note the oboist produced was – to say the least – waveringly uncertain, Sir Thomas Beecham advised the orchestra: 'Gentlemen, take your pick.'

Hard to pronounce and play, the OBOE
(With cultured folk it rhymes with 'doughboy'
Though many an intellectual hobo
Insists that we should call it oboe).
However, be that as it may,
Whene'er the oboe sounds its A
All of the others start their tuning
And there is fiddling and bassooning.
Its plaintive note presaging gloom,
Brings anguish to the concert room,
Even the player holds his breath
And scares the audience to death
For fear he may get off the key,
Which happens not infrequently.
This makes the saying understood:
'It's an ill wood wind no one blows good.'
LAURENCE MCKINNEY (born 1891); quoted in *The Frank Muir Book* (1976)

When an oboist in an orchestra that Rossini was conducting played F sharp instead of F, Rossini corrected him, and then added: 'As regards the F sharp, don't worry about it. We'll find somewhere else to fit it in.'

'All first oboists are gangsters. They are tough, irascible, double-reed roosters, feared by colleagues and conductors.'

HARRY E. DICKSON, *Gentlemen, More Dolce Please* (1969)

If you're not a musician you may have wondered if all that cacophony of tuning up before a live concert is really necessary. On the other hand, you may enjoy it. There is the story, for instance, of a rather important Asian statesman who, having attended a gala concert in London, was asked which part of the programme he liked best. 'The beginning,' he replied. 'Just before the man with the stick came in.'

Useful advice from Sir Thomas Beecham to a pedantic player: 'Forget about bars. Look at the phrases, please. Remember that bars are only the boxes in which music is packed.'

'To White Hall; and there in the Boarded Gallery did hear the musick with which the King is presented this night by Monsieur Grebus, the Master of his Musick: both instrumental (I think twenty-four violins) and vocall: an English song upon Peace. But, God forgive me! I never was so little pleased with a concert of music in my life. The manner of setting of words and repeating them out of order, and that with a number of voices, makes me sick, the whole design of vocall musick being lost by it.'

SAMUEL PEPYS, *Pepys' Diary* (1 October 1667)

This world is a difficult world, indeed,
And people are hard to suit,
And the man who plays on the violin,
Is a bore to the man with the flute.

WALTER LEARNED, *Consolation*; quoted in *The Penguin Dictionary of Modern Humorous Quotations* (1986)

Schoenberg's advice to would-be composers: 'Write what is POSSIBLE for the instruments, not what is PROBABLE.'

Quoted in H. H. Stuckenschmidt, *Schoenberg, His Life, World and Work* (translated by Humphrey Searle, 1977)

'Never having thought of writing for the guitar, I asked Julian [Bream] for a chart which would explain what the guitar could do. I managed to write some rather pretty pieces for him, except that the first six notes of the first piece all need to be played on open strings. So when he begins to play, the audience will probably think he's tuning the bloody thing up.'

WILLIAM WALTON (1902–83); quoted in *Chambers Music Quotations* (1991)

[135]

'The following amusing incident happened the other day at Burnley in connection with the examinations of the College of Violinists, now in progress. Youth of about fourteen, up for examination for graduate, played fairly well and answered questions put to him rather smartly:

Examiner: "Now, please, tell me the relative major of the scale of G minor."

Candidate (somewhat puzzled): "B, sir."

Examiner: "B what?" (after a while repeating the question, tapping the desk with his pencil)

Secretary (who happened to be in the room, overlooking the paperwork of the candidates, muttering to himself): "Be quick!"

Candidate (quite loud): "Be quick, sir."'

The Violin Times (15 July 1894)

'God save me from a bad neighbour and beginner on the fiddle.'

Italian proverb

'I am not fond of the violincello: ordinarily I had just as soon hear a bee buzzing in a stone jug.'

GEORGE BERNARD SHAW, *The World* (1890)

'The cello is like a beautiful woman who has not grown older, but younger with time, more slender, more supple, more graceful.'

PABLO CASALS; quoted in *Time* (29 April 1957)

'The cello is not one of my favourite instruments.
It has such a lugubrious sound, like someone
reading a will.'

> Attributed to the writer and broadcaster IRENE THOMAS
> (born 1920); quoted in *Bloomsbury Dictionary of Quota-*
> *tions* (1991)

'The double bass is a dangerous rogue elephant.'

> CHARLES VILLIERS STANFORD (1911); quoted in *The*
> *Guinness Dictionary of More Poisonous Quotes* (1992)

On the BBC's *Music Club* in 1954, Gerard Hoffnung
(1925–59) explained his relationship with the tuba.
It began one day as he was out walking with his
wife: 'As we passed a second-hand shop, there in the
window stood the one thing which I had wanted to
own and play ever since I could remember. There it
stood: fat, solid, charming in every way – a tuba! The
next I knew was that I had bought him, and my wife
and I were carrying him across Piccadilly Circus in the
pouring rain. At home we gave him a nice bath and
a rub. For the next three days I produced a series of
noises so dreadful and so sordid that a rumour went
about in the neighbourhood that we were keeping a
live elephant in the bath. But on the fourth day I was
able to make some quite nice noises ...'

Fiddle, *n*. An instrument to tickle human ears by friction
of a horse's tail on the entrails of a cat.'

> AMBROSE BIERCE, *The Devil's Dictionary* (1911)

'The evil that men do lives after them. The saxophone was made in 1846.'

> Asheville Times; quoted in The Guinness Dictionary of More Poisonous Quotes (1992)

'The saxophone is a long metal instrument bent at both ends. It is alleged to be musical. The creature has a series of tiny taps stuck upon it, apparently at random. These taps are very sensitive; when touched they cause the instrument to utter miserable sounds, suggesting untold agony. At either end there is a hole. People, sometimes for no reason at all, blow down the small end of the saxophone, which then shrieks and moans as if attacked by a million imps of torture.'

> London Daily News (1927)

'Harpists spend half their time tuning and the other half playing out of tune.'

> IGOR STRAVINSKY; quoted in The Guinness Dictionary of More Poisonous Quotes (1992)

'Trombones are too sacred for frequent use.'

> FELIX MENDELSSOHN; quoted in Chambers Music Quotations (1991)

'Many a sinner has played himself into heaven on the trombone, thanks to the [Salvation] Army.'

> GEORGE BERNARD SHAW, Major Barbara (1905)

Conductor Hans von Bülow to a trombonist: 'Your tone sounds like roast beef gravy running through a sewer.'

An old, old chestnut among orchestral players is the one about the trombone player who, at the end of rehearsals, shut up a fly in his music-copy. Coming to the smudge the next time he had to play that particular passage, the trombonist ran down the scale, and afterwards said: 'I don't know what that big note was, but I played it.' Hearing this story, W. S. Gilbert asked: 'Are you sure it was a fly? It might have been a bee flat.'

'His idea of heaven is eating paté de foie gras to the sound of trumpets.'

> Quoted in *The Smith of Smiths* (1934), HESKETH PEARSON's biography of the clergyman, essayist and wit Sydney Smith (1771–1845)

[Although there is some dispute about exactly whose idea of heaven it is, the image it produces is, nonetheless, an extraordinary one.]

'The tuba is certainly the most intestinal of instruments, the very lower bowel of music.'

> PETER DE VRIES (born 1910), *The Glory of the Hummingbird* (1974)

'My bowels shall sound like an harp.'
ISAIAH, 16:11

'A musical instrument-maker of Bremen was on the point of failure, and his creditors watched him so close, that he could not get a pin's worth carried away. He bethought himself of a singular stratagem for deceiving his watchmen. He got together about a hundred and fifty musicians, his friends in the shop, and set them all playing there, the overture of the 'Gazza Ladra' [Rossini's *Thieving Magpie*]. As it was night, at each movement of the orchestra, he contrived to throw some article of furniture from the back window, and the fall was so managed, that, from the noise of the instruments, no one perceived it. At last, to finish the affair so happily begun, at the end of the concert, each musician went out with his instrument. The artist went out last, and locked the shopdoor, leaving nothing to his creditors but a bust of Ramus.'

WILLIAM HONE, *The Table Book* (1835)

In *The Devil's Dictionary*, Ambrose Bierce offers this lucid comment about the lyre (probably the instrument on which Emperor Nero 'fiddled' while Rome burned):

Lyre, *n.* An ancient instrument of torture. The word is now used in a figurative sense to denote the poetic faculty, as in the following fiery lines of the great poet, Ella Wheeler Wilcox (1850–1919):

I sit astride Parnassus with my lyre
And pick with care the disobedient wire.
The stupid shepherd lolling on his crook
With deaf attention scarcely deigns a look.
I bide my time, and it shall come at length
When, with Titan's energy and strength,
I'll grab a fistful of strings, and O,
The world shall suffer when I let them go!

Staying with the lyre, Hone's *Table Book* (1835) cites
the following comforting tale: 'Sultan Amurath, that
cruel prince, having laid siege to Bagdad, and taken
it, gave orders for putting thirty thousand Persians
to death, notwithstanding they had submitted, and
laid down their arms. Among the number of these
unfortunate victims was a musician. He besought the
officer, who had the command to see the sultan's
orders executed, to spare him but for a moment,
while he might be permitted to speak to the emperor.
The officer indulged him with his entreaty; and,
being brought before the emperor, he was permitted
to exhibit a specimen of his art. Like the musician
in Homer, he took up a kind of psaltry resembling
a lyre, with six strings on each side, and accompanied
it with his voice. He sung the taking of Bagdad, and
the triumph of Amurath. The pathetic tones and
exulting sounds which he drew from the instrument,
joined to the alternate plaintiveness and boldness of his
strains rendered the prince unable to restrain the softer

emotions of his soul. He even suffered him to proceed until, overpowered with harmony, he melted into tears of pity, and relented of his cruel intention. He spared the prisoners who yet remained alive, and gave them instant liberty.'

Sir Thomas Beecham once asked a trombonist if he was 'producing as much sound as possible from that quaint and antique drainage system which you are applying to your face?'

Among the most oft-quoted comments attributed to both Beecham and Toscanini is this one to an unfortunate cellist during an orchestral rehearsal: 'Madam, you have between your legs an instrument capable of giving pleasure to thousands – and all you can do is scratch it.'

Critic's Choice

'A stir was created at a concert by the Philharmonic Trio in Wigmore Hall, when James Whitehead, cellist, walked off the stage after playing only a few bars of Webern's String Trio, op.20. Exclaiming, "I can't play this thing," Mr Whitehead quitted the stage ... He said that it was "a nightmare – not music at all, but mathematics." The majority of musicians will doubtless agree with him.'

London dispatch in *Musical Courier*, New York (May 1938)

'A good melody is such a one as would grind about the streets upon the organ.'

THOMAS ARNE (1710–78); quoted in Michael Kelly, *Reminiscences* (1826)

A squeak's heard in the orchestra,
The leader draws across
The intestines of the agile cat
The tail of the noble hoss.

GEORGE T. LANIGAN, *The Amateur Orlando* (c.1880)

'The manner of the conveyance of sounds, which is as it were the basis of music, is unintelligible. For what can be more strange, than that the rubbing of a little *Hair* and *Cat-gut* together, should make such a mighty alteration in a Man that sits at a distance?'

JEREMY COLLIER (1650–1726), *An Essay of Musick* (1702) [Incidentally, and for the benefit of cat-lovers, the mention of catgut there is part of a common misconception: catgut has never been made from the intestines of cats, but from the intestines of certain other animals, particularly sheep.]

'Is it not strange that sheeps' guts should hale souls out of men's bodies?'

WILLIAM SHAKESPEARE, *Much Ado About Nothing* (1598) Act II sc.3

'In came a fiddler — and tuned like fifty stomach-aches.'

CHARLES DICKENS (1812–70), *A Christmas Carol* (1843)

'There's many a good tune played on an old fiddle.'

SAMUEL BUTLER, *The Way of All Flesh* (1903)

'When a man is not disposed to hear music, there is not a more disagreeable sound in harmony than that of the violin.'

RICHARD STEELE (1672–1729), *The Tatler* (1 April 1712)

Another tale from Hone's *Table Book*, this time about a cellist: 'The Rev. Mr. B—, when residing at Canterbury, was reckoned a good violincello player; but he was not more distinguished for his expression on the instrument, than for the peculiar appearance of feature whilst playing it. In the midst of the adagios of Corelli or Avison, the muscles of his face sympathised with his fiddlestick, and kept reciprocal movement. His sight, being dim, obliged him often to snuff the candles; and, when he came to a bar's rest, in lieu of snuffers, he generally employed his fingers in that office, and lest he should offend the good housewife by this dirty trick, he used to thrust the *spoils* into the sound-holes of his violoncello. A waggish friend resolved to enjoy himself "at the parson's expense", as he termed it; and, for that purpose, popped a quantity of gunpowder into B's instrument. Others were informed of the trick, and of course kept a respectable distance. The tea equipage being removed, music became the order of the evening; and, after B— had tuned his instrument, and drawn his stand near enough to snuff his candles with ease, feeling himself in the meridian of his glory, he dashed away at Vanhall's 47th. B— came to a bar's rest, the candles were snuffed, and he thrust the ignited wick into the usual place; *fit fragor*, bang went the fiddle to pieces, and there was an end of harmony that evening.'

'These three take crooked ways: carts, boats, and musicians.'

    Hindu proverb

Critic's Choice

'His [Stravinsky's] "Symphony for wood instruments" was written in memory of Debussy; if my own memories of a friend were as painful as Stravinsky's seem to be, I would try to forget him.'

    ERNEST NEWMAN; quoted in *The Guinness Dictionary of Poisonous Quotes* (1991)

Bassoon, *n.* A brazen instrument into which a fool blows out his brains.

    AMBROSE BIERCE, *The Devil's Dictionary* (1911)

'The chief objection to playing wind instruments is that it prolongs the life of the player.'

    GEORGE BERNARD SHAW; quoted in *Chambers Music Quotations* (1991)

'I understand the inventor of the bagpipes was inspired when he saw a man carry an indignant, asthmatic pig under his arm. Unfortunately, the man-made sound never equalled the purity of the sound achieved by the pig.'

ALFRED HITCHCOCK; quoted in *The Guinness Dictionary of More Poisonous Quotes* (1992)

When a lady asked Sir Thomas Beecham to recommend a fairly simple instrument for her son, he told her: 'The bagpipes, Madam, for they sound exactly the same when you have finished learning them as when you first started.'

'A true gentleman is someone who knows how to play the bagpipes – but doesn't.'

ANON; a similar comment is made about that equally unfortunate instrument, the accordion

'I find distance lends enchantment to bagpipes – for example, the piper on one mountain, the listener on another.'

WILLIAM BLEZARD; quoted in *The Guinness Dictionary of More Poisonous Quotes* (1992)

'An air played on the bagpipes, with that detestable, monotonous drone of theirs for the bass, is like a tune tied to a post.'

LEIGH HUNT (1784–1859)

If the accordion and the bagpipes are among the most unloved instruments, the lugubrious bassoon is perhaps the most comic – in both sound and appearance. Not for nothing did Paul Dukas (1865–1935) cast 'the joker of the orchestra', as the bassoon is sometimes known, in the leading role in his symphonic scherzo *The Sorcerer's Apprentice* (1897).

'The bassoon in the orchestra plays the same role as Gorgonzola among cheeses – a figure of fun. Actually the bassoon can be the most romantic and passionate of instruments and Gorgonzola can be the finest of cheeses – but they must both be treated properly.'

> CECIL GRAY (1891–1951), *Notebooks* (edited by Pauline Gray, 1989)

'In the orchestra, percussion instruments are effective in inverse proportion to their number.'

> CHARLES VILLIERS STANFORD; quoted in *Chambers Music Quotations* (1991)

Clarionet, *n.* An instrument of torture operated by a person with cotton in his ears. There are two instruments that are worse than a clarionet – two clarionets.

> AMBROSE BIERCE, *The Devil's Dictionary* (1911)

[Incidentally, the same comment about two clarinets being worse than one has been made about most other instruments, particularly the flute, the saxophone, and the viola.]

'What can yield a tone so like an eunuch's voice as a true cornet pipe?'

> ROGER NORTH (1653–1734), *The Musicall Gramarian* (1728)

'When the young men serenaded, only the flute was forbidden. Why, I asked. Because it was bad for the girls to hear the flute at night.'

> ERNEST HEMINGWAY (1898–1961); on the customs of the Abruzzi in *A Farewell to Arms* (1929)

'The flute is not an instrument which has a good moral effect – it is too exciting.'

> ARISTOTLE (384–322 BC), *Politics*

'The sound of the flute will cure epilepsy and sciatic gout.'

> THEOPHRASTUS (*c.*370–*c.*288 BC); pupil, collaborator, and successor of Aristotle

'The most singular spit in the world is that of the Count de Castel Maria, one of the most opulent lords of Treviso. This spit turns one hundred and thirty different roasts at once, and plays twenty-four tunes, and whatever it plays, corresponds to a certain degree of cooking, which is perfectly understood by the cook. Thus, a leg of mutton *à l'Anglaise*, will be excellent at the 12th air; a fowl *à la Flamande*, will be juicy at the 18th, and so on. It would be difficult, perhaps, to carry farther the love of music and gourmandizing.'

> HONE, *The Table Book* (1835)

Critic's Choice

'Snickers became guffaws when Anton von Webern's Symphony for Chamber Orchestra was played. The program note spoke of "tonal pointilism", "tonal fractions" and "differentials". What the audience heard suggested odd sounds in an old house when the wind moans, the floors creak, the shades rustle, and the doors and windows alternately croak and croon. The work had von Webern's cardinal merit of brevity.'

OSCAR THOMPSON, New York *Evening Post* (19 December 1929); quoted in Nicolas Slonimsky, *Lexicon of Musical Invective* (1965)

'When Dr [Benjamin] Franklin invented the [glass] Harmonica, he concealed it from his wife till the instrument was fit to play; and then woke her with it one night, when she took it for the music of angels.'

LEIGH HUNT (1784–1859), *Autobiography*, 'Musical Memories' (1850)

'To use a woman or a guitar, one must know how to tune them.'

Spanish proverb

'"Strings for ever!" said little Jimmy. "Strings alone would have held their ground against all

the newcomers in creation. But clar'nets was death."
("Death they was!" said Mr Penny.) "And harmoniums,"
William continued in a louder voice, and getting
excited by these signs of approval, "harmoniums and
barrel organs ... be miserable – what shall I call 'em –
miserable—". "Sinners," suggested Jimmy, who made
large strides like the men and did not lag behind like the
other little boys. "Miserable machines for such a divine
thing as music!'"

> THOMAS HARDY (1840–1928),
> *Under the Greenwood Tree* (1873)

'Hang the harpers wherever found.'

> QUEEN ELIZABETH I (1533–1603), Proclamation of 1603;
> quoted in Boyle, *The Irish Song Tradition* (1976)

'A man cannot make the viola agreeable to me.
It is the only instrument which women can play
supremely well.'

> SIR THOMAS BEECHAM; speech at the Savoy, quoted in
> *News Review* (22 August 1946)

[For more comments about the viola and violists, see
page 153]

> Music is but a fart that's sent
> From the guts of an instrument.

ANON

'What a violinist! He's been asked to join the Bournemouth Symphony Orchestra – by the Glasgow Symphony Orchestra!'

Critic's Choice

'The violin is no longer played; it is pulled, torn, drubbed. The Adagio is again on its best behaviour, to pacify and to win us. But it soon breaks off to make way for a finale that transfers us to a brutal and wretched jollity of a Russian holiday. We see plainly the savage vulgar faces, we hear curses, we smell vodka. Friedrich Vischer once observed, speaking of obscene pictures, that they stink to the eye. Tchaikovsky's Violin Concerto gives us for the first time the hideous notion that there can be music that stinks to the ear.'

Neue Freie Presse, Vienna (5 December 1881)

'Each of these musicians is a soloist in his own right. If you don't believe me listen to what happens when they try and play together!'

'The most perfect expression of human behavior is a string quartet.'

JEFFREY TATE (English conductor, born 1943); quoted in *The New Yorker* (30 April 1990)

Definition of a string quartet: a Russian symphony orchestra after a tour in the West.

At a performance given by an Italian string quartet, George Bernard Shaw's companion whispered approvingly, 'They've been playing together for twelve years.' 'Surely,' said Shaw, 'we have been here longer than that.'

'The Detroit Quartet played Brahms last night. Brahms lost.'

ANON critic; quoted by Bennett Cerf, *Try and Stop Me* (1943)

The pianist Moriz Rosenthal was coerced into attending a recital by a third-rate string quartet. When the ordeal was over, the second violinist hurried over to the maestro to hear his opinion. 'What do you think?' he asked. In spite of himself, Rosenthal answered: 'Excellent.' 'Really?' asked the violinist. 'Yes,' said Rosenthal. 'And what about our tempi?' the violinist persisted, 'what did you think of them?' 'Brilliant,' said Rosenthal, 'brilliant – especially yours.'

'There is nothing, I think, in which the power of art is shown so much as in playing on the fiddle. In all other things we can do something at first. Any man will forge a bar of iron, if you give him a hammer; not so well as a smith, but tolerably. A man will saw a piece, and make a box, though a clumsy one; but give him a fiddle and a fiddle-stick, and he can do nothing.'

SAMUEL JOHNSON

'Musicians, like orthodox economists, are, on their own pet subject, vegetable cretins.'

> KAIKHOSRU SHAPURJI SORABJI (1892–1988); from comments about Stravinsky's *Les Noces*; quoted in *The English Weekly* (1949)

Flute *n.* A variously perforated hollow stick intended for the punishment of sin, the minister of retribution being commonly a young man with straw coloured eyes and lean hair.

> AMBROSE BIERCE, *The Devil's Dictionary* (1911)

Definition of a true musician: when he hears a lady singing in the bathoom – he puts his ear to the keyhole.

'Ah music! What a beautiful art! But what a wretched profession!'

> Attributed to GEORGES BIZET (1867); quoted in *Chambers Music Quotations* (1991)

And finally, the viola . . .

No one seems to know where the 'viola' joke began, but it's almost certain it started with viola players. Just as Irishmen tell the best Irish jokes and you cannot tell a good Jewish yarn unless you're from that tradition, so the best viola gags I've ever heard come from – you've guessed – the men and women who play that instrument. Some of them are really vicious (the jokes that is, not necessarily the players, though you never know!). In this section you'll be able to discover some interesting facts about this 'instrument of mixed sex . . . this hermaphrodite of the orchestra', as Beecham called it. For instance, the instrument's range, the difference between it and a violin (or even an onion), and how to tell when a violist is playing out of tune. It's just possible that viola players are hoping that some day soon they'll get their own back and we'll all start again on the saxophone gags and the drummer jokes: what's the definition of a drummer? Someone who hangs round with a band. And the story of the man begging in the streets of Manhattan: 'Spare a dollar, pal, we're collecting money to help bury a saxophonist'. Pal searches in pocket, comes up with a green-back and says: 'Here's ten bucks, bury ten of them'.

Why is it wrong for violists to take up mountaineering? Because if they get lost, it takes ages before anyone notices that they're missing.

How do you stop your violin from being stolen? Hide it in a viola case!

What do a viola and a lawsuit have in common? Everyone is happy when the case is closed.

Did you hear about the violist who dreamt he was playing at the Last Night of the Proms? He woke up to find that he was.

How many musicians does it take to play a viola? None – they wouldn't touch it.

A violist once came upon a shepherd on a country road. He stopped the shepherd and asked: 'If I can guess how many sheep you have and say the correct number, will you give me one of your sheep?' To the shepherd this sounded a bit silly, but he had many sheep and he thought it would be impossible to guess exactly, so he said, 'All right.' The violist said immediately '295'. The answer was correct; the shepherd was stunned. But he handed over one of the animals in his flock. The violist thanked him, and was about to continue on his way when the shepherd said: 'You're a violist, aren't you?' 'Well … yes,' said the violist. 'How do you know?' And the shepherd replied: 'Give me back my dog and I'll tell you.'

How do you get a violin to sound like a viola? Sit in the back and don't play.

A conductor and a violist are standing in the middle of the road. Which one do you run over first, and why? Answer: 'The conductor.' Reason: 'Business before pleasure.'

An American orchestra had just arrived in Europe for a two-week tour. One hour before the first concert, the conductor became very ill and was unable to conduct. Suddenly the orchestra had to find a substitute, but although the orchestra manager asked everyone in the orchestra whether they could step in and conduct, they all said no. All, that is, except the last chair violist. The manager was very nervous about this. 'We can't audition you,' he said. 'No problem,' replied the violist. The manager continued: 'But there's no time to rehearse. You'll have to do the concert cold.' 'No problem,' said the violist again, 'it'll be fine.' And so the violist conducted the concert, and it was a huge success. Since the conductor remained ill for most of the duration of the tour, the violist conducted all the concerts – at each one receiving standing ovations and rave reviews. Finally the conductor recovered and as he returned to take his rightful place, so the violist returned to his rightful place at the back of the viola section. As he sat down, his stand partner asked: 'Where've you been for the last two weeks?'

How is lightning like a violist's fingers? Neither one strikes in the same place twice.

A violinist noticed that at the end of each rehearsal break one of the violists would look at the inside flap of his jacket before he sat down to resume rehearsal. This procedure continued for several decades, and naturally the violinist became quite curious. One hot day, before going off on a break, the violist took off his jacket and hung it over the back of his chair. The violinist waited until everyone had left the platform, then sneaked over to the violist's jacket. Pulling back the flap, he saw a little note pinned on the inside. It read: 'viola left hand, bow right.'

What's the difference between a violin and viola?
  — A viola burns longer.
  — A viola holds more beer.
  — You can tune a violin.

We all know that a viola is better than a violin because it burns longer. But why does it burn longer? It's usually still in the case.

On a whim, a man went into a novelty shop and immediately saw an item that caught his fancy. It was a stuffed rat. The man couldn't take his eyes off it, and finally asked how much it cost. 'Forty-nine ninety-five,' said the shopkeeper, then added, 'but if for any reason you're not satisfied you can't return it.' Although the customer thought this a bit odd, he was really taken by the stuffed rat, and so he bought it. As he left the shop and headed down the street with his purchase, several live rats started following him. He thought this was strange, but nevertheless kept walking. Within a few blocks, the rats behind him had swelled to a huge pack, and the man began to be frightened. Fortunately, at that moment, he came to the river, and suddenly in fear of his life he threw the stuffed rat into the river, and to his surprise and relief all the live rats jumped into the river and drowned. The man returned immediately to the novelty shop. As soon as he walked in, the shopkeeper said: 'I told you, whatever the reason, you can't return the stuffed rat!' 'No, no!' said the man. 'I don't want to return it! I was just wondering: do you have any stuffed violists?'

Tired of all the jibes and insults, a violist decides to change instruments. So he goes into a shop and says: 'I want to buy a violin.' The man behind the counter looks at him for a moment, then says: 'You must be a viola player.' The violist is astonished. 'That's amazing,' he said, 'but how did you guess?' And the man behind the counter replied: 'This is a fish and chip shop.'

How can you tell when a violist is playing out of tune? The bow is moving.

If you throw a violist and a soprano off a cliff, which one will hit the ground first?
    — The violist. The soprano will have to stop halfway down to ask directions.
    — On the other hand, who cares?

Why don't violists play hide and seek? Because no one will look for them.

Noticing a violist crying and screaming at the oboe player sitting directly behind him, the conductor asked: 'What are you so upset about?' The violist replied: 'The oboist reached over and turned one of the pegs on my viola, and now it's all out of tune!' The conductor asked: 'Don't you think you're overreacting?' 'I'm not overreacting!' cried the violist. 'He won't tell me which one!'

What's the definition of 'perfect pitch'? Throwing a viola into a rubbish skip without hitting the rim.

What's the difference between a viola and an onion? No one cries when you cut up a viola.

Why do violists stand for long periods outside people's houses? They can't find the key and don't know when to come in.

Timmy came home from school one day very excited: 'Mummy, Mummy, guess what? Today we learned the alphabet, and I was the only one who could do the whole thing without missing any!' 'That's wonderful, dear,' said his mother, 'it's because you're a violist.' The next day, Timmy came home even more excited: 'Mummy, Mummy, guess what? Today we counted to a hundred, and I was the only one who didn't miss any numbers!' 'That's wonderful, dear,' said his mother,

'but you know, it's because you're a violist.' The day
after that, Timmy came home almost beside himself
with excitement: 'Mummy, Mummy, guess what?
Today we measured ourselves, and I was the tallest one
in the class! Is that because I'm a violist?' 'No, dear.
That's because you're twenty-seven years old.'

What's the range of a viola? As far as you can kick it.

What's the difference between a viola and a coffin?
The coffin has the dead person on the inside.

Virtually virtuosi
VIOLINISTS AND OTHER SOLOISTS

I F YOU WERE PUT TO IT ON PAIN OF YOUR LIFE, you'd probably plump for the piano as the most popular instrument. True, as has been said, it's a harp in a box and it is of course a stringed instrument on its side, but by and large throughout most westernised civilisations, with the possible exception of the fiddle, it's the piano most of us will hear first as children and, come to think of it, probably most soothingly as we head for the hoped-for peaceful oblivion of wherever we're all going next. Here's a chance to meet some of the performers of instruments other than the piano: the fiddle obviously takes pride of place as do those who have graced it with their performance. There are a few surprises here too: for instance, how does the great Karsh of Ottawa, one of the twentieth century's finest photographers, get into a volume of anecdotes about music? And while you're reading about performance, have at the forefront of your mind the perils which daily face the performer. Remember, for instance, the poor violinist who, spotting George Bernard Shaw at a recital where the violinist was struggling, tried to get the great GBS on his side: 'Ah! Mr Shaw,' he said as the audience fell silent, 'what would you like me to play next?' Shaw stood up slowly, stroked his big bushy beard and said: 'Dominoes'.

[163]

Kreisler and a friend were deep in conversation as they walked down a street in New York one morning. As they passed a fish stall, an alarm bell sounded in the violinist's memory. For a moment he couldn't think why, and – pausing in his conversation – he turned back to the stall for a second glance. Suddenly the serried ranks of fish with their slack, gaping mouths and dull staring eyes explained everything. 'My God!' he said, seizing his companion's arm. 'That reminds me – I'm playing at a concert this afternoon!'

Belgian violin virtuoso Henri Vieuxtemps (1820–81) once offered the following advice: 'Never lend your wife or your violin. Both are sure to come back damaged.' Was he speaking from experience?

On one of the several occasions the French violinist Jacques Thibaud visited London, he was asked to reveal the secret of his wonderful vibrato. With a smile, he replied: 'It is your beautiful Scotch whisky'.

On the subject of whisky, it's said that after Stravinsky took up permanent residence in the United States, he developed such an appreciation of the drink, that he is once said to have remarked: 'So much I like to drink Scotch that sometimes I think my name is Igor Stra-whisky.'

Once on tour in Russia, the violinist Jacques Thibaud struck up an acquaintance with a beautiful young woman on the Trans-Siberian Express. While the train rolled on through the endless countryside, they lunched together, dined together, and – as one thing led naturally to another – spent the night together in her compartment.

The following morning Thibaud bade his companion a contented farewell, then made his way back to where his own compartment should have been. Only it wasn't there anymore; neither was the coach in which it had been located, or several of the other coaches. A hasty inquiry revealed the problem – and his plight. At some time during his amorous night, Thibaud's part of the train had been uncoupled and sent off on another line, leaving the hapless dressing-gowned violinist stranded en route to somewhere in Siberia, sans clothes, sans documents, and sans violin.

'A virtuoso is a musician ... with real high morals.'
From a Canadian grade school essay on classical music

The violinist Jascha Heifetz once rented a summer cottage at Lake Placid in the Adirondacks in New York State. In a nearby cottage an aspiring pianist played her piano daily and badly. One morning a stranger knocked on her door. 'I'm the piano tuner,' he announced. 'I didn't order a piano tuner,' said the woman. 'No,' replied the man, 'Mr Heifetz did.'

'It was loud in spots and less loud in other spots, and it had that quality which I have noticed in all violin solos of seeming to last much longer than it actually did.'

P. G. WODEHOUSE, *The Mating Season* (1949)

Lexicographer Dr Johnson had little time for music, and when an acquaintance tried to impress upon him the difficulty of a particular passage a celebrated violinist was playing, Johnson answered: 'Difficult, do you call it, sir? I wish it were impossible.'

In 1962, Heifetz accepted the post of professor of music at the University of Southern California in Los Angeles. When questioned why he had changed direction at this stage in his career, Heifetz replied: 'Violin-playing is a perishable art. Unless it is passed on as a personal skill, it is lost.' Then he added, 'And I remember my old violin professor in Russia. He said that someday I would be good enough to teach.'

During one of his masterclasses at the university, Heifetz criticised the sound that a young student was producing as she attempted a particular piece by Bach. To illustrate how it should sound, he took up his Stradivarius, and, of course, played the piece celestially. The poor student, not unnaturally, was overwhelmed. 'That's so beautiful,' she stammered. 'But you've got to admit,' she added, 'it's different for you. For one thing, you have a Stradivarius and I've only got this old thing.' Without a word, Heifetz picked up the student's 'old thing' and proceeded to repeat the piece with exactly the same magical effect as before. When he had finished, he handed the young woman's violin back to her, and said merely: 'So?'

'I'd *never* buy a Stradivarius. I've heard he's stopped making spare parts for them.'

In his autobiography *Am I Too Loud?* Gerald Moore tells a salutary tale about the problems of excess, particularly in a land where you may not be used to the local food. It concerns the Belgian violinist Eugène Ysaÿe, who 'found himself one morning in Torquay, Devon, in company with the pianist Raoul Pugno. He had been there before and, wanting to show off his local knowledge, he took his friend to a pub and ordered two pints of raw cider. Pugno repaid the compliment and then they repaired to their hotel for lunch. It was substantial – for they were both big men – and the pianist thought the lunch was over until Ysaÿe said, "And now a wonderful surprise for you. Garçon! Bring ze Devonshire cream." A large dish was placed in the centre of the table, but Ysaÿe seized it, put it in front of him and said with commanding dignity to the amazed waiter, "And one for my friend." The couple devoured their Devonshire cream *au naturelle* with soup spoons. Their concert had to be cancelled. Devonshire cream and cider may both be indigenous to Devon but they do not make good bedfellows.'

Critic's Choice

'The violin is no longer played; it is pulled, torn, drubbed ...
Tchaikovsky's Violin Concerto gives us for the first time,
the hideous notion that there can be music that stinks
to the ear.'

EDUARD HANSLICK, *Neue Freie Presse*, Vienna (5 December
1881); quoted in *They Got it Wrong: The Guinness Dictionary of
Regrettable Quotations* (1995)

The French composer Claude Debussy fancied himself as
a music critic, and to enable him to express his sometimes
harsh opinions without revealing his true identity, he
invented an alter ego called Monsieur Croche (literally,
Mr Quaver). Combining wit and audacity, Croche –
'the dilettante-hater' – became hugely successful. Among
his less cruel comments was this one on virtuosi: 'The
attraction of the virtuoso for the public is very like that
of the circus for the crowd. There is always the hope that
something dangerous may happen: M. Ysaÿe may play the
violin with M. Colonne on his shoulders; or M. Pugno
may conclude his piece by lifting the piano with his
teeth ...'

'You know, the critics never change: I'm still getting the
same notices I used to get as a child. They tell me I play
very well for my age.'

MISCHA ELMAN, one-time child prodigy; quoted in his
seventies in Antony Hopkins, *Music all around Me* (1968)

'Everybody is talking of Paganini and his violin. The man seems to be a miracle. The newspapers say that long streamy flakes of music fall from his string, interspersed with luminous points of sound which ascend the air and appear like stars. This eloquence is quite beyond me.'

THOMAS BABINGTON MACAULAY (1800–59); letter (1831)

'When playing at Lord Holland's someone asked him [Paganini] to improvise on the violin the story of a son who kills his father, runs away, becomes a highwayman, falls in love with a girl who will not listen to him, leads her to a wild country spot and suddenly jumps with her from a rock into an abyss where they disappear forever. He listened quietly and, when the story was at an end, asked that all the lights should be extinguished. He then began playing, and so terrible was the musical interpretation of the idea that had been given to him that several ladies fainted and the salon, when relighted, looked like a battlefield.'

LOUIS ENGEL, *From Mozart to Mario* (1886)

'I have wept only three times in my life: the first time when my earliest opera failed, the second time when, with a boating party, a truffled turkey fell into the water, and the third time when I first heard Paganini play.'

GIOACHINO ROSSINI, quoted in Jeffrey Pulver, *Paganini: The Romantic Virtuoso* (1936)

When Schoenberg was informed that his violin concerto was so difficult it would need a soloist with six fingers, the composer is said to have replied: 'I can wait.'

Still on the virtuosity of Paganini, *Fuller's Anecdotes* quotes the following story from a certain Sam Ward: 'The master held a guitar across his lap. "Your young friend is musical?" enquired he. "Fanatico!" replied Gear. "Then, he shall hear me practice for tomorrow night's concert." Taking the guitar he converted that little-understood instrument into an orchestra of bewildering and harmonic sonority. Now it seemed a battle, with the clash of swords, shouts of combatants, the roll of the drum. Then wails of pain and grief appeared to emerge from the sounding board over which his fingers flew like what the Westerners call "greased lightning". The performance lasted perhaps half an hour, and the dampness of his dishevelled locks indicated the intensity of the emotion and the exertions that expressed it. When the maestro received, with a sad smile, our frantic applause, I inquired whether he was going to rehearse on the violin his programme for the morrow. He shook his head: "I never rehearse the violin. My practice is the gymnastics of the guitar, to be sure of my suppleness of finger and delicacy of touch. My violin never fails me."'

Two of the world's greatest violinists, Jascha Heifetz and Mischa Elman, were dining together in a restaurant much frequented by musicians – including their principal rival Fritz Kreisler. Scarcely had they sat down than their

waiter approached with an envelope. Heifetz glanced
at the inscription on the envelope which read: 'To the
World's Greatest Violinist', then picked it from the
tray and handed it across the table. 'Something for you,
I think, Mischa.' Elman read the envelope, and handed
it back. 'No, no, Jascha, this is surely for you.' In this
fashion the note passed back and forth a few times, until
finally Elman was persuaded to open the envelope. He
did so, drew out the enclosed letter, unfolded it, and read:
'Dear Fritz.'

'In respect to violins, I am polygamous.'
    FRITZ KREISLER

Among the distinguished audience for Jascha Heifetz's
triumphant American début at New York's Carnegie
Hall in 1917 were violinist Mischa Elman, and the pianist
Leopold Godowsky (1870–1938). As the sixteen-year-old
Heifetz played to increasingly spellbound admiration,
Elman became increasingly restless and fidgety, frequently
pulling at his collar and mopping his forehead. Finally
he nudged Godowsky: 'Awfully hot in here, don't you
think?' 'Not for pianists,' replied Godowsky.

The violinist Isaac Stern (born 1920) was once introduced
to Muhammad Ali (born 1942) at a New York party.
'You might say we're in the same business,' said Stern,
'we both earn a living with our hands.' With the lightning
speed for which he was renowned, Ali replied: 'You must
be good, there isn't a mark on you.'

'The Italian composer and violinist Archangelo Corelli (1653–1713) was requested one evening to play, to a large and polite company, a fine solo which he had lately composed. Just as he was in the midst of his performance, some of the number began to discourse together a little unreasonably; Corelli gently laid down his instrument. He was asked if there was anything the matter with him. Nothing, he replied, he was only afraid that he interrupted conversation.'

> John Mainwaring (c.1724–1807), *Memoirs of the Life of the Late George Frederic Handel* (1760)

[A selection of similar tales about interruptions appears on page 114–6.]

In the original *Oxford Companion to Music* (1938), Percy Scholes writes about a tiff between the Polish violinist Henryk Wieniawski (1835–80) and Anton Rubinstein. For some reason, during a tour together in the United States in 1872, one virtuoso received better billing than the other. From that moment on, though the two played the 'Kreutzer' Sonata side by side more than seventy times, they never exchanged another word.

In *Karsh: A Fifty-Year Retrospective*, the distinguished photographer Yousuf Karsh recalls photographing Pablo Casals – unusually with his back to the camera: 'I was so moved on listening to him play Bach that I could not for some moments attend to photography. I have never posed anyone else facing away from the camera, but it seemed just right.

Years later when the photograph was on exhibition at the Museum of Fine Arts in Boston, I was told that every day an elderly gentleman would come and stand for many minutes in front of it. Full of curiosity, a curator finally inquired gingerly, "Sir, why do you come here and stand in front of this picture?"

He was met with a withering glance and the admonition, "Hush, young man. Can't you see I am listening to the music!"'

'Kreisler plays as the thrush sings in Thomas Hardy's poem, hardly conscious of his own lovely significance.'

NEVILLE CARDUS, *The Delights of Music* (1966)

In his invaluable *A General History of Music*, the 18th-century music historian Charles Burney quotes the Greek orator and satirist Lucian (*c*.117-*c*.180) on the first and last appearance of an unfortunate flautist: 'Harmonides, a young flute-player and scholar of Timotheus, at his first public performance began his solo with so violent a blast that he breathed his last breath into his flute, and died upon the spot.'

Critic's Choice

'Tchaikovsky's Violin Concerto is a very uneven work. The Finale is nothing less than music run mad, a frenzy of notes of incomprehensible savagery.'

Boston *Herald* (14 January 1893); quoted in Nicolas Slonimsky, *Lexicon of Musical Invective* (1979)

This story, quoted in G. T. Ferris, *The Great Violinists and Pianists* (1881), concerns the Italian violinist and composer Giovanni Battista Viotti (1755–1824), and Ferdinand Langlé, a professor of harmony in the French Conservatoire, and an intimate friend of Viotti: 'One charming summer evening the two were strolling on the Champs Elysées. They sat down on a retired bench to enjoy the calmness of the night, and became buried in reverie. But they were brought back to prosaic matters harshly by a babel of discordant noises that grated on the sensitive ears of the two musicians. They started from their seats, and Viotti said:

"It can't be a violin, and yet there is some resemblance to one."

"Nor a clarinet," suggested Langlé, "though it is something like it."

They approached the spot whence the extraordinary tones issued, and saw a poor blind man standing near a miserable-looking candle and playing upon a violin made of tin-plate.

"Fancy!" exclaimed Viotti, "it *is* a violin, but a violin of tin-plate! Did you ever dream of such a curiosity!" and, after listening a while, he added, "I say, Langlé, I must possess that instrument. Go and ask the old blind man what he will sell it for."

Langlé approached and asked the question, but the old man was disinclined to part with it.

"But we will give you enough for it to enable you to purchase a better," he added; "and why is not your violin like others?"

The aged fiddler explained that his good, kind nephew Eustache, who was apprenticed to a tinker, had made it.

"Well," said Viotti, "I will give you twenty francs for your violin. You can buy a much better one for that price; but let me try it a little."

He took the violin in his hands, and produced some extraordinary effects from it. A considerable crowd gathered around, and listened with curiosity and astonishment to the performance. Langlé seized on the opportunity, and passed round the hat, gathering a goodly amount of chink from the bystanders, which, with the twenty francs, was handed to the astonished old beggar.

"Stay a moment," said the blind man, recovering a little from his surprise; "just now I said I would sell the violin for twenty francs, but I did not know it was so good. I ought to have at least double for it."

Viotti had never received a more genuine compliment, and he did not hesitate to give the old man two pieces of gold instead of one, and then immediately retired from the spot. He had scarcely gone forty yards when he felt someone pulling at his sleeve; it was a workman, who politely took off his cap, and said:

"Sir, you have paid too dear for that violin; as it was I who made it, I can supply you with as many as you like at six francs each.'"

In the middle of a recital with Rachmaninov, Fritz Kreisler suffered a lapse of memory. Edging close to the piano, he whispered urgently: 'Where are we?' Rachmaninov's reply was to the point: 'Carnegie Hall.'

While on a visit to some friends of the family, the child prodigy Mischa Elman was invited to demonstrate his talent. 'For an urchin of seven, as I was at that time,' he recalls, 'I flatter myself I rattled off Beethoven's "Kreutzer" Sonata finely.' However, the 'Kreutzer' has several long rests, and during one of these, a motherly old lady in his audience patted him on the shoulder and said sweetly, 'Play something you know, dear.'

'Artists who say they practise eight hours a day are liars or asses.'

> ANDRÉS SEGOVIA (1980); quoted in *The Guinness Dictionary of Poisonous Quotes* (1991)

'The acclaimed musician Johann Peter Salomon gave violin lessons to George III, but found the king neither an apt nor a diligent pupil. Torn between exasperation and the wish to encourage the royal fiddler, Salomon delivered the following pronouncement: "Your Majesty, fiddlers may be divided into three classes: the first, those who cannot play at all; the second, those who play badly; the third, those who play well. You, sire, have already attained the second class."'

> FRANCIS W. GATES (1898)

A pupil of Casals was playing a cello piece that she knew very well and, indeed, had performed on many occasions. Halfway through, however, her mind went blank. She struggled to remember, and finally was able to continue. Afterwards, Casals told her: 'Good! Everything should be new every time you play it.'

Jascha Heifetz acquired a new secretary, who was effusive in his compliments every time the violinist played. Finally, Heifetz told him that he didn't need to be constantly complimented. 'If I play well,' he said, 'I know it myself. If I don't, I shall only be disappointed if you flatter me.' Hoping to please, the secretary obeyed Heifetz to the letter, and after the next concert – a particularly successful one – he remained completely silent. Heifetz stormed up to him. 'What's the matter? You don't like music?'

At a vaudeville show once, Heifetz was mesmerised as an acrobat performed a series of tricks at the same time as playing the violin: he played the instrument upside down, he played it behind his back, he played it standing on his head, he even played it turning somersaults. Eventually Heifetz turned to his companion and whispered: 'Why doesn't he play it straight?'

In *Facing the Music* (1973), the American conductor and violinist Henri Temianka writes about an unusual solution to an all too common problem. It concerns the cellist Gregor Piatigorsky. As a teacher, he was finding it impossible to get through to him about how a particular piece of music should sound. Again and again he played the piece to the student, but there was no improvement. If anything, the student's playing got worse. Thinking about the problem one morning, Piatigorsky wondered if – by playing the piece with his customary flair – he might not be putting the student off. So he began to fumble and make mistakes. And from that moment on the student's playing began to improve dramatically. Finally, the date arrived for the student's graduation, and, as now expected, he performed brilliantly and passed with flying colours. At a reception afterwards, as the great cellist struggled through the throng of proud parents to congratulate his ex-pupil, he overheard someone ask the young man what he thought of Piatigorsky. 'As a teacher, excellent,' he replied, 'but as a cellist, lousy.'

As a composer of 'household' and minstrel songs in America, Stephen Foster (1826–64) was unrivalled. A self-taught musician, he was also a popular and accomplished flautist. According to Humphrey Laning in *The Humor of Music and other Oddities in the Art*, he was once invited to an important party, and suspecting that his invitation was more for his musical talents than his company, he sent his flute to the party, while he stayed at home.

In a similar vein, the Spanish violinist and composer Pablo Martín Melitón de Sarasate y Navascuéz received an invitation to a grand dinner, or rather to dine 'with your violin'. Knowing that he would be asked – expected – to play for his hostess's guests, Sarasate replied that he would be delighted to come, 'but my violin does not dine'.

In *Memories and Impressions*, Helena Modjeska relates about the perils of playing to salon audiences. The soloist on this occasion was the Polish violinist Henryk Wieniawski. The music mentioned was a popular piece at the time by the Swiss composer Joseph Joachim Raff (1822–82):

'Once in London he was invited by some person of high rank to play at his house. When he stepped out to the front, all eyes and lorgnettes were on him, and there was not even a murmur in the audience; everybody was still and attentive; but he scarcely struck the first notes of Raff's Cavatina, when all the people in the room began to talk. It was very provoking, and he was determined to teach them a lesson: knowing that every English man and woman had to rise and be silent when the hymn "God save the Queen" was played, he gave a wink to the accompanist, then passed cleverly from Raff to the tune of the hymn and played it fortissimo. To his great satisfaction, the people stopped talking, and those who were seated rose to their feet. But when he resumed the Cavatina, they also instantly resumed their talk. He again intoned the hymn and gained a few minutes of silence, but the noise was stronger than ever when he changed the tune. He repeated the hymn trick five or six times. When he finished no one understood the hint; they only wondered at the strange composition in which the national hymn was so often repeated.'

'I occasionally play works by contemporary composers, and for two reasons. First, to discourage the composer from writing any more, and secondly to remind myself how much I appreciate Beethoven.'

JASCHA HEIFETZ, *Life* (28 July 1961); quoted in *Handbook of 20th Century Quotations* (1984)

When, towards the end of his long and distinguished career, Sarasate was visited by a famous music critic who declared him a genius, Sarasate frowned and shook his head, almost sadly. 'A genius!' he sighed. 'For thirty-seven years I've practised fourteen hours a day, and now they call me a genius!'

On an American tour, violinist Henryk Wieniawski gave a recital in a half-empty auditorium in Boston. In spite of the disappointing attendance, he was immediately offered a return engagement. 'Thank you, but no,' he said. 'I'll get out of the habit of playing in public.'

Already is too loud

CONDUCTORS AND CONDUCTING

'I'VE A SOFT SPOT FOR CONDUCTORS,' a musician friend of mine once told me, 'it's a bog in the West of Ireland and I'd like to put most of them in it!' It seems that in the past conductors have taken a leaf from Dr Johnson's reflection on the Irish, when he remarked they were a very fair race . . . 'they never speak well of each other'. Beecham on Sargent was as rude as possible. Well aware of Sir Malcolm Sargent's nickname 'Flash Harry', when Beecham heard his rival was to tour Japan, he muttered: 'Ah! Flash in Japan!' And then as a punchline he once remarked that Herbert von Karajan was a 'sort of musical Malcolm Sargent'. Ouch! Come with us into this section and next time you meet one of the white tie-and-tails brigade you'll be the measure of them. Better still, use them as social smoothers to infiltrate musicians, since most of the performers I know remind me of the trumpet player who phoned his orchestra's secretary twenty times one morning to ask how the conductor, who was in hospital, was getting on. Fed up after so many calls, the secretary screamed: 'I've told you nineteen times, he died last night.' 'I know,' replied the trumpet player, 'but I just love hearing you say it!'

From 1934 to his death, Fritz Busch (1890–1951) conducted the Glyndebourne Opera in its summer season of Mozart and other operas. Among his attributes, Busch was noted for accuracy and decisiveness, and he demonstrated both of these at his very first rehearsal with the Glyndebourne orchestra. He raised his baton to begin, and then – before a single note had been played – lowered it again, and announced quietly: 'Already is too loud.'

One of the musical world's greatest conductors, Arturo Toscanini, was almost as famous for his tantrums as for his technique. (According to legend, some of his orchestral players even kept pictures of the scowling conductor to show to their children, warning them that if they misbehaved he would be round to see them.) During one of his more violent furies at rehearsal, Toscanini snatched his gold watch from its chain, threw it to the floor and stamped on it. At their next rehearsal, the players presented him with a cheap nickel watch, on which was engraved: 'For Maestro – for Rehearsal Purposes Only'.

Sharing a cab with a colleague in New York, Beecham kept whistling the same passage from a Mozart concerto, over and over and over again. Finally, his colleague could stand it no longer. 'Must you do that?' he exclaimed. 'My dear fellow,' Beecham replied, 'you may be able to hear only my whistling, but I can hear the full orchestra.'

An anonymous critic once wrote somewhat harshly of
George Szell: 'He has an enormously wide repertory. He
can conduct anything provided it's by Beethoven, Brahms,
or Wagner. He tried Debussy's *La Mer* once. It came out
as *Das Merde*.'

'We cannot expect you to be with us the whole time,' said
Beecham somewhat caustically to a player who was having
trouble following the beat, 'but perhaps you would be
kind enough to keep in touch now and again?'

During his time in charge of German opera at the
Metropolitan Opera in New York in the early years
of this century, conductor Alfred Hertz (1872–1942)
developed the disconcerting habit of waiting till long
after the orchestra had finished tuning before making
his entrance. This had the effect of worrying the
audience, and making them wonder if something was
drastically wrong, so that when finally he did appear the
enthusiastic applause was more of relief than anything
else. In an effort to dissuade Hertz from the practice, the
following notice was placed in his dressing-room: 'Am
I not always on time? Yes, I am not.' Either the subtlety
was lost on Hertz, or he just ignored it, but the practice
continued. The management tried another tack. At that
time, the orchestra pit in some European opera houses
was concealed by a wooden hood. This helped to focus
attention on the stage. A similar hood was tried at the
Met. Hertz soon discovered that 'making an entrance'
was entirely wasted on a audience who couldn't see him,

and gave up the practice. Because it muffled the music, the hood was eventually removed, but by then Hertz had taken the point.

For a time Anton Schindler (1795–1864) acted as Beethoven's secretary. He was also his first biographer. Here he describes the composer's conducting: 'He had ears only for his composition and was ceaselessly occupied by what gestures he could employ to indicate the desired expression. To suggest a diminuendo, he would crouch lower and lower, and at a pianissimo he would almost creep under the desk. When the volume of sound grew, he rose up as if out of a stage-trap until he stood upon the tips of his toes almost as big as a giant, waving his arms and as if about to soar upwards to the skies.'

In his *Peacocks on the Podium*, Charles Neilson Gattey describes the rather unorthodox conducting methods of Gaspare Spontini (1774–1851). In addition to unusual military-style commands to the orchestra – barked sometimes in a confusing mixture of German, French and his native Italian – Spontini used, instead of a baton, an ebony cosh with a solid ivory ball at each end, which he grasped in the middle. Later in life, when his sight became so poor he could not even see a baton, he claimed to direct the orchestra solely with his eyes: 'My left eye is trained on the first violins, my right on the second violins, and if the eye is to have power, one must not wear glasses, as so many bad conductors do, even if one is shortsighted like I am ... All the same I can make the troops play as I want, merely by fixing them with my eyes.' Perhaps it's just as well that orchestras in those days were much smaller than today.

Until the early nineteenth century, if there was any conducting to be done it was either with the hand, a roll of manuscript paper (including the score itself), or the violin bow or 'fiddlestick'. The first modern baton is said to have been introduced into England by the German composer, violinist and conductor Louis Spohr at a Philharmonic Society concert in London in 1820. Apparently, one of the guarantors of the Society was so disturbed by Spohr's innovation that he attempted to have it banned. But the baton was too useful and effective, and over the next fifty years it became the standard instrument of conducting.

One musician who did not use a baton, but no doubt wished he had, was Jean-Baptiste Lully (1632–87), musician to the court of Louis XIV. To celebrate his majesty's recovery from a serious illness in 1686, Lully composed a *Te Deum* (a Latin hymn of thanksgiving to God). In those days it was standard for the conductor to beat time on the ground with a stick. In Lully's case, the stick was a large, heavy wooden staff. Conducting the first performance of his *Te Deum* in January the following year, he missed the ground and struck his big toe instead. The heavy blow led to painful swelling, which in turn led to an unpleasant abscess. This was followed by gangrene, and then death.

[187]

Describing Sir Georg Solti's conducting of *The Marriage of Figaro*, a critic wrote: 'He conducted the second act finale with a smile on his face – it would have been better if he had cut his throat.'

Quoted in *The Guinness Dictionary of More Poisonous Quotes* (1992)

As a conductor, Hector Berlioz was an eccentric, if not excessive, showman. In 1840, he marched through the streets of Paris conducting his *Grande symphonie funèbre et triomphale* with a sword. His players there were a full orchestra and a military brass band of two hundred. At a concert a few years later, he conducted Beethoven's Fifth Symphony with thirty-six double basses, Weber's overture to *Der Freischütz* with twenty-four French horns, and *Moses' prayer* (from Rossini's *Moses in Egypt*) with twenty-five harps. His orchestra on that occasion numbered more than a thousand players. Eleven years later, at the close of the Paris Exhibition on 15 November 1855, he premièred *L'Impériale*, a celebratory cantata dedicated to Napoleon III, performed by an orchestra, military band and chorus of 1200, and conducted by himself and five assistants. He described the performance as 'apocalyptic', and said that his giant orchestra transported him 'into the valley of Jehosaphat!'

'As far as the public is concerned, there are only two golden rules for a good performance. And that is for the orchestra to begin together and to end together. As for what goes on in between, the public doesn't give a damn.'

SIR THOMAS BEECHAM

'If you want to please only the critics: don't play too loud, too soft, too fast, too slow.'

ARTURO TOSCANINI

Beethoven was completely deaf by the time he finished his last symphony, the Ninth or 'Choral' Symphony, in 1824. Nevertheless, he was persuaded to help conduct the work at its première. Accordingly, he stood before the orchestra during the performance and at the beginning of each of the four movements indicated the tempo. When the symphony was over and the last chord had been played, the audience rose as one and cheered, cried 'Bravo!', applauded and stamped their feet. Beethoven, however, was unaware of all the noise, until at last one of the soloists tugged at his sleeve and gestured to the audience. Beethoven turned to see the ovation he could no longer hear, and bowed.

When a trumpet player incurred Toscanini's displeasure during a rehearsal, the maestro shouted in frustration: 'God tells me how he wants this music played – and you stand in his way!'

During a rehearsal of the orchestra of the Städtische Oper in Berlin, the conductor Leo Blech (1871–1958) noticed that one of the players was having trouble following his beat. 'You're new here?' asked Blech. The player replied that he was. 'Well,' said Blech, 'there is a problem here, but we can work on it till it's all right.' And for the next hour he did work on the problem until there was none. 'There!' said Blech. 'It's fine now, and at the concert tonight you'll sound perfect.' 'Tonight?' said the player, 'but I won't be here tonight. I'm only helping out with rehearsal this morning.'

'If anyone has conducted a Beethoven performance, and then doesn't have to go to an osteopath, then there's something wrong'.

SIR SIMON RATTLE (born 1955), *The Guardian* (31 May 1990)

'You know why we conductors live so long? Because we perspire so much.'

SIR JOHN BARBIROLLI

Exasperated by the way his orchestra played at rehearsal one day, Toscanini suddenly exclaimed: 'After I die, I am coming back to earth as the doorkeeper of a bordello, and I won't let you in, not a one of you!'

'I spend up to six hours a day waving my arms about, and if everyone else did the same they would stay much healthier.'

SIR MALCOLM SARGENT

On the subject of energy and exertion, there is of course the (no doubt) apocryphal story of the conductor who handed his featherweight baton (14.175g, 0.5oz) to a heavyweight boxer and challenged him to see how long he could move it around as though conducting. The boxer did not last as long as he thought he would.

Halfway through a rehearsal of César Franck's latest work, the symphonic poem *Les Djinns*, the conductor Edouard Colonne turned to the composer and asked: 'You like this?' Franck replied that he was delighted. 'Well,' said Colonne, turning back to the orchestra, 'it's all frightful music, but we'll go on with it anyway.'

Early in his career, Russian-born Sergei Koussevitsky was hugely successful as a virtuoso double bass. Later, he turned to conducting, and eventually became resident conductor of the Boston Symphony Orchestra. And again he was hugely successful – at least as far as the audience was concerned. Unfortunately for the players in his orchestra, Koussevitsky's beat was at best erratic and at worst downright confusing – especially when beginning a piece. To clarify his position, Koussevitsky once advised the orchestra: 'When my stick touches the air, you play.' Finally, the players discovered the real answer: the downbeat was when Koussevitsky's hand passed the third button on his waistcoat!

'Conducting is the only job that can be learnt in an evening.'
    SIR ADRIAN BOULT

Late in his life, Otto Klemperer was attending a lecture given by the German composer Paul Hindemith. It was a long lecture, and when at last it ended, Hindemith asked if there were any questions. For a moment, it seemed as though there would be none, until finally Klemperer dragged himself to his feet to ask, 'Where is the lavatory?'

The wife of a player in the Hallé Orchestra discovered her husband was having an affair with another member of the orchestra. Tearfully she went to the Hallé's conductor, Sir John Barbirolli, poured out her heart, and asked for his advice. Barbirolli was sympathetic, gave her a fatherly hug and a pat on the shoulder, and told her: 'My dear, there's nothing really to worry about. It'll all blow over.' And then he added: 'Besides, he's playing better than ever.'

'Conductors' careers are made for the most part with "romantic" music. "Classic" music eliminates the conductor; we do not remember him in it.'
    IGOR STRAVINSKY; quoted in Robert Craft, *Conversations with Igor Stravinsky* (1958)

Toscanini's memory was legendary, as was his ability to conduct without the score. Once, when rehearsing the Philharmonic in César Franck's Symphony, he interrupted the proceedings and accused the clarinettist of playing a wrong note. The clarinettist denied the 'wrong note', and repeated the passage from his score.
    'No, no!' Toscanini insisted. 'You are playing A flat.

That is the wrong note. It should be A.' To prove that he
was playing the correct note, the clarinettist took his part
to the podium. Toscanini peered at the page momentarily,
and then declared: 'This is an error!' The full conductor's
score was sent for, it arrived, he opened it, and proved
to the clarinettist that the part-copyist had copied it
wrongly.

An even more extraordinary example of Toscanini's
memory is demonstrated in this anecdote about a
clarinettist (possibly the same one), who approached
Toscanini shortly before a concert, and said: 'Maestro, I
cannot play tonight. My E flat key is broken.' Toscanini
thought deeply for a moment and then announced, 'It's all
right, you can play. You don't have that note in your part
tonight.'

Three years before his death at the age of 89, Pierre
Monteux signed a twenty-five-year contract as chief
conductor of the London Symphony Orchestra – with an
option of renewal for another twenty-five years!

Never the most confident of composers, Anton Bruckner
was badly affected by the poor reception of both his
Second and Third symphonies. So when Hans Richter
rehearsed and conducted the première of his Fourth
Symphony ('The Romantic') in Vienna, with great feeling
and understanding, he was especially grateful – in fact, so
much so that he tipped the conductor an Austrian thaler.

'Take this,' he said, 'and drink my health in a mug of beer.' Richter was deeply touched by the gesture. He kept the coin and wore it ever after on his watch chain 'as a memento of the day on which I wept'.

At a dress rehearsal of Rimsky-Korsakov's *Mozart et Salieri*, relations were none too smooth between the Russian bass Fyodor Chaliapin, who wanted the tempo one way, and the conductor, who wanted it another. After enduring Chaliapin's gestures and stampings for some time, the conductor at last felt obliged to make a stand. 'Mr Chaliapin,' he said, 'kindly remember that I am the conductor.' As far as Chaliapin was concerned, this was no defence, and he replied: 'In a garden where there are no birds a croaking toad is a nightingale.' To such an insult there is no comeback. The conductor laid down his baton, closed his score and, with as much dignity as he could muster, walked out.

At Covent Garden, Sir Thomas Beecham was conducting an unexceptional opera that required a horse. As the action reached a strident climax, the audience's attention was distracted as the horse, in full view, offered his own contribution to the proceedings. 'My God!' muttered Sir Thomas. 'A critic!'

After many years of conducting the heavyweights of opera such as Verdi and Wagner at the Met and La Scala (not to mention the on- and offstage temperaments

that inevitably went with the job), Toscanini turned
to the concert works of early romantic composers
such as Beethoven and Schubert. When an old
friend bumped into him in New York one day,
and remarked with surprise on how very well the
conductor was looking, Toscanini exclaimed: 'Five years
without opera!'

Toscanini once declared that he first kissed a woman and
first smoked a cigarette on the very same day, and had
never had time for tobacco since.

Conductor Luigi Arditi (1822–1903), once renowned for
his waltz song 'Il Bacio' ('The Kiss'), went to Rossini
to settle a dispute about the English horn solo in his
overture to *William Tell*. While Arditi remembered it
going such a way, some of his players insisted that
they had always played it another way. Taking a card,
Rossini wrote out the correct way, inscribed it 'To the
author of "Il Bacio"', and signed it. The next time
an English horn presumed to be an expert on *William
Tell*, Arditi proudly presented his autographed authority
and settled the matter there and then. He wrote in
his memoirs: 'Need I say, that it was not without
considerable satisfaction?'

Reviewing one of Malcolm Sargent's concerts in
Australia, the critic of *The Age*, Felix Werder, wrote: 'Here
is an Englishman who feels with his head and thinks with
his heart.'

In *Talks with Great Composers*, Arthur Abell describes a symphony concert in Weimar in 1889 at which he joined the resident conductor of the Weimar Orchestra, Eduard Lassen, in his box to hear Richard Strauss conduct the first performance of his own *Don Juan*. Knowing how Lassen loathed modern music, he was therefore not particularly looking forward to the 'indignation and even hisses' that would undoubtedly follow the performance. To his amazement, however, Lassen's reaction was completely the opposite: the conductor shouted 'Bravo! Bravo!' and applauded vigorously. Totally mystified, Abell said: 'Herr Kapellmeister, I am astonished at seeing you applaud *Don Juan* so enthusiastically. I was under the impression that you detested the work.' 'I do detest it most emphatically,' Lassen replied, and then explained: 'I am not applauding *Don Juan*, I am applauding Strauss. He is a great conductor. He is only twenty-six years old and I am sixty. I have been conducting the Weimar Orchestra for twenty-nine years and Strauss has been here only one, but he produces greater effects with the musicians than I have ever been able to achieve. Strauss is a genius and I am only a talent.'

Riding high on the success of 'The Blue Danube', Strauss travelled to the United States for a series of concerts. Among his performances was one in Boston on 17 June 1872 in front of an audience of a hundred thousand. His orchestra numbered 2000 players (including 350 violins), and his choir 20,000 singers. To help them all keep the beat, Strauss was armed with a long, illuminated baton, and a hundred assistant conductors. 'A cannon shot sounded — a gentle hint for the two thousand to commence playing', he wrote later. 'I gave my signal, my hundred assistant conductors followed me as swiftly as they could, and there then broke out an unholy racket, such as I will never forget.'

'"Great" conductors, like "great" actors, soon become unable to play anything but themselves.'

    IGOR STRAVINSKY, *Themes and Conclusions* (1972)

After the last of the many telegrams, cards and letters from composers, conductors and musicians, had been read out congratulating him on his seventieth birthday, Sir Thomas Beecham asked: 'What, nothing from Mozart?'

'I am not a fascist. I hate Tchaikovsky and I will not conduct him. But if the audience wants him, it can have him.'

    PIERRE BOULEZ; quoted in J. Peyser, *Boulez: Composer, Conductor, Enigma* (1976)

'Second trumpet, you're too loud!' complained Beecham at a rehearsal one morning. 'I'm sorry, Sir Thomas,' said the leader, 'but the second trumpet telephoned to say he's going to be a little late.' Quick as ever, Beecham replied: 'Well, when he arrives tell him he's too loud.'

Keen to impress an orchestra with his aural powers, an up-and-coming conductor sneaked into the library one evening, took the double-bass part of the score he was due to rehearse the following day, and pencilled in a wrong note. Came the rehearsal the next morning, the conductor stopped the orchestra at the appropriate point and said knowingly: 'Fourth double bass, you played a B flat. You should have played B natural!' 'Of course I should, and I did,' said the player, 'but some bloody idiot pencilled in a flat.'

Sir Malcolm Sargent was rehearsing a Strauss waltz with the BBC Symphony Orchestra. When a player muttered 'too fast', Sargent rounded on him: 'Too fast? Only last night I danced a waltz with the Queen Mother.'

At the end of yet another exhausting season of Promenade Concerts, Sir Henry Wood was complimented on his physical fitness. His ritual of a poached egg and half a glass of mineral water before a concert was well known, but what about after? 'No secret,' Wood answered. 'I go home, have a good supper, half a bottle of wine, and a cigar. Not like X,' he continued, mentioning a young conductor. 'What does he do? Goes home and drinks hot milk. Milk makes you so . . . adagio.'

'It is easy to be a conductor. All you have to do is play the notes.'

ARTURO TOSCANINI; quoted by Ethan Mordden, *Opera Anecdotes* (1985)

Perceived as the conductor's expert on Verdi, Toscanini was often approached by younger members of the profession for advice. When one of these was preparing *Il Trovatore* for performance and asked Toscanini how to choose the proper tempo for the 'Anvil' Chorus, the Maestro replied: 'Just listen to the women doing their laundry by the river. They get it right every time.'

During a brief spell in San Francisco, André Previn had the opportunity to study with Pierre Monteux, who at that time was music director of the San Francisco Symphony. In his autobiography *No Minor Chords*, Previn describes an occasion a few years later when Monteux watched him conducting a provincial orchestra. 'He came backstage after the performance. He paid me some compliments and then asked, "In the last movement of the Haydn symphony, my dear, did you think the orchestra was playing well?" My mind whipped through the movement; had there been a mishap, had something gone wrong? Finally, and fearing the worst, I said that yes, I thought the orchestra had indeed played very well. Monteux leaned toward me conspiratorially and smiled. "So did I," he said. "Next time, don't interfere!" It was advice to be followed forever . . .'

'In the first movement alone I took notice of six pregnancies and at least four miscarriages.'

> SIR THOMAS BEECHAM about Bruckner's Seventh Symphony; quoted in Harold Atkins and Archie Newman, *Beecham Stories* (1978)

For Joan Sutherland's role in a recording of *Messiah* in 1961 (to be conducted by Sir Adrian Boult), her husband, the conductor Richard Bonynge, wrote a new cadenza for her to sing. She forgot to inform Sir Adrian of the addition, and at the first rehearsal the cadenza took him completely by surprise. 'Ah,' he muttered, '"The Mad Scene" from Handel's *Messiah*.'

Beethoven once gave a performance of a new piano concerto in which he forgot that he was the soloist and began to conduct instead. At the first sforzando he threw out his arms so vehemently that he knocked both candlesticks off the piano. The audience burst out laughing, which enraged Beethoven. He made the orchestra start all over again. To avoid a repetition of the accident, two boys from the chorus were recruited to stand holding the lights on either side of Beethoven. Unfortunately, when it came to the sforzando, Beethoven again flung out his arms. One of the boys, keeping a wary eye on the maestro, had seen what was coming and had managed to duck. The other boy was not so lucky, and received Beethoven's hand full in the mouth, which made him stagger and drop the candlestick. The audience's laughter now so enraged Beethoven that he hit the keyboard with his fist and broke half a dozen piano strings!

'There are no good or bad orchestras, only good or bad conductors.'

'Technique is communication: the two words are synonymous in conductors.'

LEONARD BERNSTEIN; quoted in *The Times* (27 June 1989)

Hans Knappertsbusch (1888–1965) disliked rehearsing anything he'd conducted before. His philosophy on the subject was simple: 'You know the piece,' he would say to the orchestra, 'I know the piece, so why rehearse it?' On one occasion, however, he found he had to rehearse, and at the performance that evening the music did not go as well as it usually did. When at last it was over, Knappertsbusch left the podium grumbling: 'Wouldn't have happened if we hadn't had that — rehearsal.'

The Indian conductor, and former pianist and violinist Zubin Mehta (born 1936) was once asked to name his favourite orchestra. He thought for a moment and then replied diplomatically: 'Would a devout Muslim answer as to which of his wives he preferred? One can have preferences about details only – a dimple here, an oboe there.'

'You played F sharp there,' the conductor complained to a bassoonist. 'It should be F natural.' Disconcerted not one jot, the bassoonist replied: 'It was F natural when it left here.'

Sir Thomas Beecham conducted a concert in London in honour of the aged Saint-Saëns. The principal piece was the composer's Third Symphony (the 'Organ' Symphony). Both Beecham and the players found the tempi drearily slow. With the composer in the audience Beecham was careful not to speed up, though he did manage to enliven the proceedings with some exaggerated accentuation. After the concert, he asked Saint-Saëns what he thought of his interpretation. 'I have lived many years,' the composer replied, 'I have known many conductors. And there are two kinds: one takes the music too fast, the other too slow. There is no third.'

'Show me an orchestra that likes its conductor and I'll show you a lousy conductor.'

> GODDARD LIEBERSON; quoted in *The Guinness Dictionary of More Poisonous Quotes* (1992)

A conductor, whose command of English was none too good at the best of times, once lost his temper with an errant flautist. 'Your damned nonsense can I stand twice or once,' he shouted, 'but sometimes always, by God, never.'

A bassoonist who had always wanted to conduct the orchestra was finally given his chance at a minor concert. A few days after the event, he met the chief conductor Hans Richter in the street. 'How did it go?' asked Richter. 'Very well,' the bassoonist replied, and then added, 'You know, this conducting business is really quite simple.' 'Ssh!' said Richter. 'Don't give us away, I beg you!'

During a rehearsal of Ravel's *Boléro*, Koussevitsky lost his temper with a struggling percussionist. Finally he threatened the player: 'If you make me more nervous I send you bill from my doctor.'

In *Ego* 4, the distinguished critic James Agate (1877–1947) wrote of the equally distinguished conductor Sir Landon Ronald (1873–1938): 'There was one respect in which Ronald outshone all other conductors. This was in the gleam of his shirt front and the gloss of his enormous cuffs, out of which peeped tiny, fastidious fingers. He made music sound as if it, too, was laundered.'

As well as his conducting talents, Toscanini was renowned for his verbal abuse. Once, at the Metropolitan Opera in New York, after an especially unpleasant rehearsal (even by Toscanini's standards), the members of the orchestra sent a delegation to the Met director, Giulio Gatti-Casazza. 'Never have we been called such names!' they complained. 'Ah,' replied Gatti, with a weary shrug: 'You should hear what he calls me.'

At the age of twenty-four, Malcolm Sargent became the youngest Doctor of Music in British music history. Some thirty years later he was made Sir Malcolm. On hearing the news, his rival Sir Thomas Beecham remarked: 'Been knighted, has he? It was only yesterday he was doctored.'

Otto Klemperer was once approached by the management of an Israeli concert hall and asked if he would like to conduct *Messiah* there. The conductor frowned, thought about the invitation for a moment, and then said finally: 'Tell me, was there not once some trouble with your country and the Messiah?'

Sir Thomas Beecham was once travelling by train to an important concert in the north of England. The journey had scarcely begun when an expensively dressed woman in the same non-smoking compartment opened her handbag, took out a cigarette and – as an afterthought – asked the conductor: 'You will not object if I smoke?' 'No, madam,' Beecham replied, 'and you will not object if I am sick.' Somewhat taken aback by this retort, the woman said: 'I don't think you realise who I am. I have some influence with the company that owns this railway.' 'Indeed, madam,' said Beecham. 'Indeed,' continued the woman imperiously, 'I am one of the Directors' wives.' Beecham replied: 'Madam, if you were the Director's only wife I should still be sick.'

In his day, Arthur Nikisch (1855–1922) was considered the outstanding conductor of Romantic music. Asked once for his opinion of Schoenberg's works, he threw up his hands in despair. 'If I had to conduct music of that character,' he said sadly, 'I should change my profession.'

Beecham was conducting a rehearsal of a new work by Frederick Delius, with the composer himself sitting close by. After one passage, Beecham turned to him for his response. 'Good,' said Delius, 'yes, good. Except for the horns, maybe.' Without another word to Delius, Beecham turned back to the orchestra, 'Gentlemen, we'll go from bar six again.' They repeated the passage, and when it was over, Beecham turned once again to Delius. This time the composer was completely satisfied. 'Yes, yes, that was better,' he said. 'Good,' replied Beecham, then added quietly: 'By the way, Fred, there are no horns in that passage.'

Shortly before he died in his ninetieth year, Pierre Monteux was asked about his pleasures in life. 'I have two abiding passions,' he replied. 'One is my model railway, the other, women. But, at my age, I find I am getting just a little too old for model railways.'

In 1855, the Philharmonia Orchestra in London was conducted for one season by Wagner, but he was not engaged again. Referring later to that particular season, *The Times* described it as 'one of the most disastrous on record'.

Hearing that Beecham was contemplating conducting Wagner's *Götterdämmerung* without the score in front of him, a musicologist asked how on earth he would manage the opera's extraordinarily complex rhythmical changes.

Beecham was having none of it. 'There are no rhythmical changes in *Götterdämmerung*,' he replied. 'It goes straight on from half past five till midnight like a damned old cart horse!'

Beecham had scant respect for those on the periphery of music, especially those who wrote or talked about it. 'A musicologist,' he once declared, 'is a person who can read music but can't hear it.' On Doctors of Music, he had this to say: 'Doctors of Music! That means they have sat on their bottoms for six hours and done a paper on harmony, but they can't play the National Anthem.' And as for music critics ... 'drooling, drivelling, doleful, depressing, dropsical drips.'

Following the unenthusiastic reception of a performance of Beethoven's Ninth Symphony in Berlin, the conductor Hans von Bülow turned to the audience and in a heartfelt speech rebuked them for being 'unmusical'. Then he played the symphony all over again, in order – as he put it afterwards – 'to educate the Berlin public to better things'.

After a very dull concert with a rather second-rate orchestra, the conductor found himself buttonholed by the orchestral board's chairperson. 'Tell me, Maestro,' she gushed, 'when was the last time you conducted our orchestra?' 'Tonight,' replied the conductor.

'You must have the score in your head, not your head in the score.'

HANS VON BÜLOW, remark to Richard Strauss; quoted in Harold C. Schonberg, *The Great Conductors* (1967)

'The trouble with music critics is that so often they have the score in their hands and not in their heads.'

SIR THOMAS BEECHAM; quoted in *The Guinness Dictionary of Poisonous Quotes* (1991)

During a rehearsal for Wagner's *The Mastersingers*, Malcolm Sargent attempted to improve the first clarinet's performance by persistently singing along in unison. Finally, the clarinettist had had enough: 'Sir Malcolm,' he said politely, 'if you are going to sing it, I'll stop playing it.' Sargent took the point and kept quiet.

Another conductor who liked to demonstrate by singing how a passage should go was Arthur Nikisch. Whenever an instrument had a difficult solo he would sing it over to the player, and then say simply: 'That is my idea of it, now play it how you like'.

Toscanini also sang with his orchestra, not to aid a player but simply for the sheer enjoyment of the music. Unfortunately, he was usually totally unaware of what he was doing. At Salzburg once, during a dress rehearsal, his singing (once described tactfully as a 'wordless hum') was especially noticeable above the instruments. Suddenly he brought the orchestra to a halt and demanded, 'For the love of God, who's singing here?'

On another celebrated occasion, Toscanini was completely carried away as he conducted his NBC Symphony Orchestra in a broadcast performance of Puccini's *La Bohème*. As the two impoverished artists Rodolfo and Mimì came together in 'O soave fanciulla', their impassioned avowal of love towards the end of the first act, radio listeners hearing the broadcast could not fail to wonder how the duet had suddenly become a trio. One listener – a diva, who had sung under Toscanini during his time at La Scala – knew the answer all too well. Next day she cabled Toscanini: 'DEAR MAESTRO IT WAS SO GOOD TO HEAR YOU SING AGAIN.'

And finally on the subject of singing conductors and communication, this story from Dudley Moore's *Off-beat* is worth repeating in its entirety: 'A British orchestra was rehearsing a new work by a modern French composer, under the baton of a French conductor. The maestro was unhappy with a passage being played by the clarinet. "No, no, no!" he cried. "Don't play it like that, but like this . . ." and he sang "La-la-la . . . la, la . . . laaa LA." "Ah!" said the player, in mock surprise, "you mean" . . . and also sang "La-la-la . . . la, la . . . laaa LA." "Yes, yes that's it," the conductor said, content. The clarinettist paused for a moment, then – through gritted teeth – said, "Good. Now we know we can both sing it, who's going to play it?"'

'At a rehearsal I let the orchestra play as they like. At the
concert I make them play as *I* like!'

SIR THOMAS BEECHAM; quoted in Neville Cardus, *Sir Thomas
Beecham* (1961)

Although Sir Thomas Beecham was an eager and energetic
supporter of a variety of twentieth-century music, the
compositions of Ralph Vaughan Williams were never
on his list. If anything, he was barely aware of Vaughan
Williams's music even when he had to conduct it, as
he proved unwittingly during a rehearsal of one of
the composer's symphonies. Throughout the work, he
conducted as though he were miles away. Suddenly, he
became aware that the orchestra had stopped. 'Why aren't
you playing?' he asked. 'It's finished, Sir Thomas,' said
the leader. Beecham looked down at his score, turned the
page, and finding it finished, said: 'So it is, thank God!'

'The leader of the Vienna Philharmonic once called over
to me at a rehearsal when, my baton not being at hand,
I was about to take another: "Not that one, Doctor –
that one has no rhythm".'

RICHARD STRAUSS, *Recollections and Reflections* (1949)

'For a fine performance only two things are necessary:
the maximum of virility coupled with the maximum of
delicacy.'

SIR THOMAS BEECHAM; quoted in Atkins and Newman,
Beecham Stories (1978)

Franz Strauss (1822–1905), a professional horn player and father of Richard Strauss, gives a musician's point of view: 'You conductors who are so proud of your power! When a new man faces the orchestra – from the way he walks up the steps to the podium and opens his score – before he even picks up his baton – we know whether he is the master or we.'

Quoted in Harold C. Schonberg, *The Great Conductors* (1967)

'A conductor should reconcile himself to the realization that regardless of his approach or temperament the eventual result is the same – the orchestra will hate him.'

OSCAR LEVANT, *A Smattering of Ignorance* (1940)

'Beethoven was wont to give the signs of expression to his orchestra by all manner of extraordinary motions of his body. Whenever a *sforzando* occurred, he flung his arms wide, previously crossed upon his breast. At a piano, he bent down, and all the lower in proportion to the softness of tone he wished to achieve. Then when a *crescendo* came, he would raise himself again by degrees, and upon the commencement of the *forte*, would spring bolt upright. To increase the *forte* yet more, he would sometimes shout at the orchestra, without being aware of it.'

LOUIS SPOHR, *Autobiography* (1865)

Hearing a member of the audience walk out during the performance of a modern piece he loathed conducting, Otto Klemperer exclaimed: 'Thank God someone understands it!'

In the early 1920s, Richard Strauss set down his beliefs in *Ten Golden Rules for the Album of a Young Conductor*:

'1) Remember that you are making music not to amuse yourself, but to delight your audience.

2) You should not perspire when conducting: only the audience should get warm.

3) Conduct *Salome* and *Elektra* as if they were by Mendelssohn: Fairy Music.

4) Never look encouragingly at the brass, except with a brief glance to give an important cue.

5) But never let the horns and woodwinds out of your sight. If you can hear them at all they are still too strong.

6) If you think the brass is not blowing hard enough, tone it down another shade or two.

7) It is not enough that you yourself should hear every word the soloist sings. You should know it by heart anyway. The audience must be able to follow without effort. If they do not understand the words they will go to sleep.

8) Always accompany a singer in such a way that he can sing without effort.

9) When you think you have reached the limits of prestissimo [very fast], double the pace.

10) If you follow these rules carefully you will, with your fine gifts and your great accomplishments, always be the darling of your listeners.'

From Harold C. Schonberg's *The Great Conductors* (1967)

For many years, Sir Malcolm Sargent was chief conductor of the BBC Symphony Orchestra. His contemporary, Sir Thomas Beecham, once remarked on this fact: 'The BBC Symphony Orchestra can best be described as the "Sargent's Mess!"'

'I have always maintained that I am an executant and not, and have no right to be, a critic of any kind, even to the extent of having preferences and favourites. I consider it is my job to make the best of whatever is put before me once I have agreed to conduct the work. I am often asked which is my favourite Beethoven or Brahms symphony, and I can only answer that my favourite is the one that I am at the moment performing, or studying, the one that is uppermost in my mind.'

ADRIAN BOULT, *My Own Trumpet* (1973)

Sir Thomas Beecham on Arturo Toscanini: 'A glorified bandmaster!'

In his biography *Malcolm Sargent*, Charles Reid describes the ceremonial opening of the 1948 Olympic Games in Wembley Stadium. Sargent, in charge of all the music, had drawn a huge choir from seven of London's biggest, with the stirring accompaniment of the massed bands of the Brigade of Guards. The day was very hot – which threw the instruments out of tune – and the stadium was packed. Among the musical items were the Hallelujah

Chorus, and of course the National Anthem — with the crowd invited to join in both 'at discretion'. After it was all over, Sargent was asked: 'What's it like conducting such a crowd in such a place?' He replied: 'Like taking a jellyfish for a walk on an elastic lead.'

Conductor Sir Eugene Goossens once told of a remarkably untalented amateur musician of no little musical education, who suddenly decided that as he had always wanted to be a conductor — and as he was reasonably well-heeled — he would give it a go. To that end, he hired a concert hall and a symphony orchestra. At his first rehearsal — in preparation for the launch of a great concert début — the players quickly discovered that the man knew little about conducting, and even less about how to control an orchestra. After two hours of struggling to understand his erratic gestures, the players were hot, tired and not a little irritable. Suddenly, in the middle of a slow, stately passage that was obviously not sounding quite as it should, the percussionist lost his temper and for about ten seconds took out his frustration on every instrument at his disposal. When it was all over and a sort of astonished silence descended on the hall, the conductor laid down his baton, glared at the players, and asked, 'All right, who did that?'

'I am not the greatest conductor in this country. On the other hand I'm better than any damned foreigner.'
      SIR THOMAS BEECHAM

As a conductor, Richard Strauss practised what he preached (see page 211). Under his baton, tiny by comparison with other conductors, he would despatch Beethoven's Ninth at least fifteen minutes faster than anyone else.

Barbirolli on Beecham: 'He conducted like a dancing dervish.'

Beecham on Barbirolli: 'Barbirolli has worked wonders with the Hallé. He has transformed it into the finest chamber orchestra in the country.'

'Oh! to be a conductor, to weld a hundred men into one singing giant, to build up the most gorgeous arabesques of sound, to wave a hand and make the clamouring strings sink to a mutter, to wave again, and hear the brass crashing out in triumph, to throw up a finger, then another and another, and to know that with every one the orchestra would bound forward into a still more ecstatic surge and sweep, to fling oneself forward, and for a moment or so keep everything still, frozen, in the hollow of one's hand, and then to set them all singing and soaring in one final sweep, with the cymbals clashing at every flicker of one's eyelid, to sound the grand Amen.'

J. B. PRIESTLEY; quoted in Harold C. Schonberg, *The Great Conductors* (1967)

Following a brilliant performance of *The Magic Flute*, a member of the audience approached Sir Thomas Beecham and enthused: 'Thank you so much for this wonderful evening with Mozart and Beecham.' 'Why drag in Mozart?' Beecham replied.

A few years after the London première of Strauss's *Elektra*, the Bandmaster of the Grenadier Guards made an arrangement of some of the music for brass band. Some months of practice later, the musicians performed their 'potpourri' for the first time at the Changing of the Guard at Buckingham Palace while the king, George V, was in residence there. The band had not been playing long when an urgent note from the king himself was delivered to the Bandmaster. It read: 'His Majesty does not know what the band has just played, but it is *never* to be played again.'

Beecham had just finished a tour in Australia, and was about to begin the journey home to England, when a reporter asked: 'When will you be returning to Australia?' Beecham replied: 'Does anyone ever *return* to Australia?'

'To make music is wonderful. To make great music with a fine orchestra to an audience is very wonderful. To make great music with a fine orchestra to an audience which is at times so concentrated in its attention that it's almost frightening – to express this is beyond my words. But that is how I feel about it.'

SIR MALCOLM SARGENT; speech, Last Night of the Proms in 1962

Beecham was once rehearsing a violin concerto with the soloist and full orchestra. It was the height of summer, and in the unventilated rehearsal room the atmosphere was hot and sticky. In addition to the heat, it was also after lunch. Consequently, the music produced was not of the most focused. Nevertheless, Beecham persevered, and as the spirit of the piece took hold and the orchestra's playing began to improve, he leaned over to the violinist and said: 'Don't look now, but I believe we're being followed.'

One of pianist Mark Hambourg's fondest memories was his first performance of Beethoven's Third Piano Concerto with Eugene Ysaÿe as conductor in Brussels: 'This was an exciting event because Ysaÿe became so absorbed in the beauty of the music that he forgot to continue conducting, and just stood raptly listening.'

A composer, known for his modern, dissonant music, slipped in to a rehearsal hall to listen to his latest work being conducted by Sir Adrian Boult. For some time he sat silent, but with growing impatience. Finally, he leapt to his feet. 'Excuse me, Sir Adrian!' he called. Boult greeted him pleasantly: 'Good afternoon, how nice to see you.' 'Forgive my interrupting,' said the composer, 'but couldn't you up the tempo just a bit?' Sir Adrian smiled: 'Well, yes, indeed we could. But you do realize that we haven't come to your piece yet?'

Wanting to reward a retiring general for his long and

admirable service, Czar Nicholas I of Russia asked him to choose a post at Court. The general bowed and said: 'Your Majesty, I would like to conduct the orchestra.' 'Conduct?' the Czar exclaimed. 'But you know nothing about music.' 'Anyone can wiggle a stick, Sire,' replied the general. 'It is so simple.'

Following a visit to Birmingham, the Italian composer and conductor Luigi Arditi was recommended to return to London via Stratford-on-Avon. 'It would be a pity to leave England without seeing the birthplace of the great Shakespeare,' said the friend. 'Shakespeare?' Arditi replied. 'Who is he?' His friend was astounded. 'Don't tell me you haven't heard of the man who wrote *Othello* and *Romeo and Juliet* and *The Merry Wives of Windsor*?' he asked. 'Ah,' said Arditi, 'the librettist.'

Sir Thomas Beecham was once asked if it was true that he preferred not to have women in the orchestra. 'The trouble is,' he said, 'if they are attractive it will upset my players and if they're not it will upset me.'

By the end of his career, Pittsburgh Symphony Orchestra conductor William Steinberg was completely bald. Relating an episode in his musical past, he once told an audience: 'There I was tearing my hair and . . .' Suddenly he halted, clasped his shell-like skull, and groaned, '*What am I saying?*'

During a performance of Beethoven's overture *Leonore* No.3, the off-stage trumpet twice failed to play on cue. As soon as the overture was finished, the conductor jumped down from the rostrum and stormed into the wings to have it out with the trumpeter. Instead he found the player wrestling to retrieve his trumpet from a burly stagehand. 'You can't blow that damn thing here, I tell you,' the stagehand was insisting. 'There's a concert going on.'

Halfway through a South American tour with the NBC Symphony Orchestra, Toscanini and the orchestra arrived in a town on the third of July, three days in advance of their next concert. Not surprisingly, the players, who had been on the road for some time, were looking forward to a couple of days off from rehearsals, so they were none too pleased when Toscanini called them for rehearsal the following morning. Nevertheless, they obeyed, and duly turned up the next morning. When they were ready to begin, Toscanini entered, asked them to stand, and then led them through 'The Star-Spangled Banner'. At the end, he announced: 'Today is the Fourth of July,' and then dismissed them for the rest of the day.

George Bernard Shaw once described Beecham, rather ambiguously, as 'the most adult conductor I have ever met'.

Not long after he moved to the United States, Stravinsky was conducting at an important orchestral rehearsal in Chicago. During one particular passage, the first violinist made the same stupid mistake not once or twice, but three times. In spite of his irritation, Stravinsky spoke to the player coolly and calmly, and the matter was settled. As Stravinsky left the hall after the rehearsal a Russian colleague who had observed the proceedings complimented him on his control. 'I don't know how you could be polite. I would have been so angry.' 'Ah,' Stravinsky explained in his native tongue, 'that is because I have so far learned only polite phrases in English. You should have heard what I was calling him under my breath in Russian!'

Sir Thomas Beecham was once asked if he had heard any Stockhausen. 'No,' he is said to have replied, 'but I believe I have trodden in some.'

Following a violent argument with the second trombonist, Toscanini ordered the man to leave the rehearsal. As he reached the exit, the trombonist turned and shouted: 'Nuts to you!' 'No, no!' Toscanini shouted back, 'it is too late to apologise!'

Sir Eugene Goossens (1893–1962) described the joy of conducting: 'It is the most wonderful of all sensations that any man can conceive. It really oughtn't to be allowed.'
    Quoted in Beverley Nichols, *Are They the Same at Home?* (1927)

Beecham was about to begin rehearsal one morning when he noticed an unfamiliar face among the woodwinds. 'Good morning, Mr—?' he asked. 'Ball,' replied the newcomer. 'I beg your pardon?' 'Ball, Sir Thomas.' 'Ball? Ah, *Ball*! How very singular.'

Sergei Koussevitsky held the post of conductor of the Boston Symphony Orchestra from 1924 to 1949, and was greatly admired, particularly by the female patrons of Boston's musical pride. At a reception one evening, one such lady approached him and gushed: 'Mr Koussevitsky, to me, you are a god.' 'Ah, madame,' Koussevitsky replied, 'what a responsibility!'

Sir Thomas Beecham once conducted a performance of a Beethoven piano concerto, at which the soloist's memory suddenly failed. As his playing drifted off into other works, the conductor vainly struggled to keep going. 'We started with Beethoven,' he recalled, 'and I kept up with him through the Grieg, Schumann, Bach, and Tchaikovsky. But then he hit one I didn't know, so I stopped dead.'

For eight years in the 1920s, British violinist Henry Holst held the coveted position of leader of the Berlin Philharmonic. At the time, the orchestra was under the ambiguous direction of Furtwängler. On one occasion, somebody asked Holst: 'How do you follow Furtwängler's beat?' Holst replied, 'Do we?'

Throughout his long and distinguished career, Wilhelm Furtwängler was notorious for his vagueness. Typical of this is the following instruction during a rehearsal: 'Gentlemen, this phrase must be – it must be – it must – you know what I mean. Please, try it again.'

Paul Hindemith was rehearsing one of his more dissonant orchestral compositions, when he suddenly brought the orchestra to a halt. 'No, no, gentlemen!' he exclaimed. 'It sounds wrong, yes, but it's still not right!'

Discussing with Oscar Levant the possible ways of interpreting the opening bars of Beethoven's Fifth Symphony, the composer and conductor Bernard Herrmann (1911–75) asked: 'How would you play them, Oscar?' Levant replied: 'Oh, I'd omit them.'

Following a rehearsal with the London Symphony Orchestra, André Previn was enjoying a drink with the soloist, when a young composer whose work he admired came into the bar. Previn welcomed him and offered him a drink. 'I heard your concert the other night,' the composer said. 'It sounded marvellous. It was the night the Beethoven Sixth was played in the first half.' 'Oh, God,' said Previn, 'that was the night Maurizio Pollini was scheduled to play the Fourth Piano Concerto in the second half, but at the last minute he cancelled, and we were stuck with that dreadful third-rate pianist. I'm really sorry you had to sit through that.' The young man looked thoughtfully at Previn and then said: 'I didn't mind. The pianist is my wife.'

'Every member of the orchestra carries a conductor's baton in his knapsack.'

TOM STOPPARD, *Every Good Boy Deserves Favour* (1978)

On tour in Palestine in 1937, Malcolm Sargent and the orchestra experienced more than just a little racial tension and rioting, and had to be escorted from one venue to the next in armoured cars. Following one skirmish, a report appeared in some British newspapers that Dr Sargent and his players had been ambushed. When somebody mentioned the news to Sir Thomas Beecham, he thought for a moment and then said: 'Ambushed by the Arabs, eh? I never knew they were so fond of music.'

In his collection *Off-beat*, Dudley Moore tells of the occasion Otto Klemperer stepped onto the podium, acknowledged the audience's applause, and then turned to the orchestra. Unbeknown to the conductor, an expanse of very white shirt was visible through his open fly. Dutifully, the leader of the orchestra came to the rescue. 'Maestro,' he whispered, 'your fly is undone.' Somewhat bewildered, Klemperer looked at him and then asked: 'What has that to do with Beethoven?'

In 1952, thirty-nine years after the première of Stravinsky's *Le Sacre du Printemps* ('The Rite of Spring'; see page 67), Pierre Monteux returned to Paris to conduct the work again. This time the audience was unanimous in its enthusiasm, a reaction which led Monteux to remark: 'There was just as much noise as last time, but the tonality was different.' On another occasion, however, he confessed: 'I did not like *Le Sacre* then. I have conducted it fifty times since. I do not like it now.'

Late in his life, Otto Klemperer seemed to become – on the concert platform at least – more and more eccentric. At one concert in London, for instance, he took his place on the podium, picked up his baton, raised his arms, looked at the orchestra, and then laid the baton down. Orchestra and audience awaited his next move, but there was none. Nothing happened. Finally, the leader leaned forward and asked: 'Dr Klemperer? Are you all right?' Klemperer stared at him for a moment, and then replied quietly: 'What a life!' And then he took up his baton again and began to conduct.

Till the fat lady sings

SINGERS AND SINGING

M Y FATHER, a lifelong lover of opera, didn't suffer foolish singers gladly. Listening through gritted ears one day in our home in Dublin many years ago to a seriously unimpressive soprano he was heard to mutter: 'It's time that girl's mother took her home!' An echo, of course, of opera not being over until the fat lady sings. They are unique, aren't they? Those people from all over the world who not only put themselves into the public eye in performance but have to achieve musical greatness at the same time. I remember once bumping into the actor Michael Williams at a performance of Donizetti's *L'Elisir d'Amore* at Covent Garden which starred Pavarotti. Luciano did an almost musical-hall turn with one of his arias, causing Michael to remark to me at the next interval: 'Your man can act a bit as well, eh!?'

Somewhere between my Dad and Michael Williams I'd like you to absorb that spirit as we enter the world of singing and singers.

As Wagner's opera *Lohengrin* draws to its close, a magic swan glides on to the stage drawing a boat to take the worthy hero to rejoin the fellowship of the Knights of the Holy Grail. At least that's the plan. On one occasion, however, the stage staff controlling the swan were just a little too efficient. No sooner had the swan appeared, than it began to disappear back into the wings, leaving the Danish tenor Lauritz Melchior (1890–1973) somewhat stranded. Melchior, or so the legend goes, was unfazed. He walked downstage, took out his watch, and coolly asked the audience: 'Can anyone tell me when the next swan leaves?'

Opera, *n.* A play representing life in another world, whose inhabitants have no speech but song, no motions but gestures and no postures but attitudes. All acting is simulation, and the word *simulation* is from *simia*, an ape; but in opera the actor takes for his model *Simia audibilis* (or *Pithecanthropos stentor*) – the ape that howls.

> The actor apes a man – at least in shape;
> The opera performer apes an ape.
> AMBROSE BIERCE, *The Devil's Dictionary* (1911)

On the effect of Italian opera on the London stage, Joseph Addison (1672–1719) wrote in *The Spectator* (21 March 1711): 'Nothing is capable of being well set to music that is not nonsense.'

'If any person has sung or composed against another person a song such as was causing slander or insult to another, he shall be clubbed to death.'

ROMAN LAW, Twelve Tables (449 BC)

Richard Strauss's tragic one-act opera *Elektra* is scored for a larger than usual orchestra, but for the composer attending rehearsals for the Dresden première in 1909, the sound was still not enough. This was especially evident during the scene between Elektra and her murderous mother Klytemnestra, the latter sung with her customary dramatic bravura by mezzo Ernestine Schumann-Heink. Rushing down the aisle, Strauss yelled to the conductor Ernst von Schuch, 'Louder, louder the orchestra! I can still hear the Heink!'

Conducting the London première of *Elektra* at Covent Garden in 1910, Sir Thomas Beecham had a similar thought, allegedly because he judged the quality of singing not quite up to his standard. Just before the performance he told the orchestra: 'Those singers up there on the stage think they are going to be heard. Well, we're going to make damned certain that they are not.'

In his autobiography, *Between Acts: An Irreverent Look at Opera and Other Madness,* baritone Robert Merrill (born 1917) recalls a rehearsal for a new production of *Pagliacci* in which he was cast as Silvio, the lover of young Nedda:

'Our Nedda, however, was a woman of a certain weight, about forty pounds more than mine. For our passionate duet, the director thoughtfully placed her in a chair and instructed me, "Get on your knees and put your head in her lap."

I demurred *sotto voce*, "But she doesn't have a lap."

"Well, snuggle as close as you can."

The only place my face could go was into her crotch. This evoked unsuppressed giggles from others in the cast.

"It looks bad," I told the director.

But he was determined to be creative. "These are Italian peasants, they're passionate people."

I went back to my prenatal position and we started the duet. On a lovely phrase, my voice wobbled.

"What's the trouble?" the director yelled.

"I think I'm getting an echo."'

Castrati: 'These men, who sing so well but without warmth or expression are, in the theatre, the most disagreeable actors in the world. They lose their voice at an early age and become disgustingly fat ... There are some letters, such as R, which they are quite unable to pronounce.'

JEAN-JACQUES ROUSSEAU (1712–78), *Dictionnaire de Musique* (1767)

'A singer able to sing so much as sixteen bars of good music in a natural, well-poised and sympathetic

voice, without effort, without affectation, without
tricks, without exaggeration, without hiatuses,
without hiccuping, without barking, without baa-ing
— such a singer is a rare, a very rare, an excessively
rare bird.'

    HECTOR BERLIOZ, *A Travers Chant* (1862)

'I even think that *sentimentally* I am disposed to
harmony. But *organically* I am incapable of a tune. I
have been practising "God Save the King" all my life;
whistling and humming it over to myself in solitary
corners; and am not yet arrived, they tell me, within
many quavers of it.'

    CHARLES LAMB, *Essays of Elia* (1820—23)

Lamb was certainly not disposed to music, as he was the
first to admit: 'A carpenter's hammer, in a warm summer
noon, will fret me into more than midsummer madness.
But those unconnected, unset sounds are nothing to
the measured malice of music.' He particularly disliked
Italian opera, which was at that time all the rage. 'I have
sat through an Italian opera,' he wrote in 'A Chapter on
Ears' (*Essays of Elia*, 1820—23), 'till, for sheer pain, and
inexplicable anguish, I have rushed out into the noisiest
places of the crowded streets, to solace myself with
sounds which I was not obliged to follow, and get rid
of the distracting torment of endless, fruitless, barren
attention!'

'I love Italian opera — it's so reckless. Damn Wagner, and his bellowings at Fate and Death. Damn Debussy, and his averted face. I like the Italians who run all on impulse, and don't care about their immortal souls, and don't worry about the ultimate.'

> D. H. LAWRENCE (1885–1930); letter (1 April 1911); quoted in *The Letters of D. H. Lawrence* (1979)

Sir Thomas Beecham's first venture as an operatic conductor was Ethel Smyth's *The Wreckers* at His Majesty's Theatre in London in 1909. For Beecham, the highlight was a gala performance in the presence of King Edward VII and Queen Alexandra. Following this momentous occasion, Beecham asked the king's private secretary, who had accompanied the royal party, what the king had thought about the performance. The private secretary was vague. 'Surely he said something,' Beecham insisted. 'Well, yes, he did,' the private secretary admitted finally. 'Three-quarters of the way through, His Majesty awoke suddenly and said: "Fritz, that's the fourth time that infernal noise has raised me!"'

'I don't know why it is, Tito. I don't particularly like your voice, but when you sing I forget to play.'

> An unidentified orchestra member; quoted in Tito Gobbi, *My Life* (1979)

'I like an aria to fit a singer as perfectly as a well-tailored suit of clothes.'

> WOLFGANG AMADEUS MOZART; quoted in *Chambers Music Quotations* (1991)

'I see you have a singing face — a heavy, dull,
sonata face.'

GEORGE FARQUHAR (*c.*1677–1707), *The Inconstant* (1702)
Act II sc.1

The Irish tenor John McCormack was in his dressing room
at Covent Garden preparing for a performance one evening,
when there was a knock at the door, and Caruso entered.
'Enrico!' said McCormack, surprised. 'What are you
doing here?' 'You think I allow you to walk on the stage
without I come to wish you well?' said Caruso. 'I take that
as a great compliment, coming from the world's greatest
tenor,' McCormack replied. Caruso smiled. 'Since when,
Giovanni,' he asked, 'did you become a baritone?'

'The good singer should be nothing but an able
interpreter of the ideas of the master, the composer . . .
In short, the composer and the poet are the only true
creators.'

GIOACHINO ROSSINI; letter (1851)

'I'm sure the programme will be delightful, after a few
expurgations. French songs I cannot possibly allow.
People always seem to think that they are improper, and
either look shocked, which is vulgar, or laugh, which
is worse. But German sounds a thoroughly respectable
language, and indeed, I believe is so.'

Lady Bracknell in OSCAR WILDE *The Importance of Being
Earnest* (1895) Act I

In February 1761, the evangelist and founder of
Methodism, John Wesley (1703–91), went to Drury Lane
to hear Thomas Arne's oratorio *Judith*; here he describes
his impressions in his journal: 'Some parts of it were
exceedingly fine; but there are two things in all modern
music which I could never reconcile to common sense.
One is singing the same words ten times over; the other,
singing different words by different persons, at one and
the same time. And this in the most solemn addresses to
God, whether by way of prayer or of thanksgiving. This
can never be defended by all the musicians in Europe,
till reason is quite out of date.'

[Handel's] 'oratorios thrive abundantly. For my part,
they give me an idea of heaven, where everybody is to
sing whether they have voices or not.'

    HORACE WALPOLE (1717–97); letter (1743)

The last composer to write for the castrato or male
soprano voice was Rossini's contemporary and rival
Giacomo Meyerbeer, who in 1824 composed *Il Crociato
in Egitto* for Giovanni Battista Velluti (1781–1861). Velluti
died at the ripe old age of eighty.

Italian music critic Enrico Panzacchi sums up his
enthusiasm for the last of the Vatican's male sopranos
in the late 1800s: 'What singing! Imagine a voice that

combines the sweetness of the flute, and the animated
suavity of the human larynx – a voice that leaps and
leaps, lightly and spontaneously, like a lark that flies
through the air and is intoxicated with its own flight;
and when it seems that the voice has reached the loftiest
peaks of altitude, it starts off again, leaping and leaping
still with equal lightness and equal spontaneity, without
the slightest sign of forcing or the faintest indication
of artifice or effort; in a word, a voice that gives the
immediate idea of sentiment transmuted into sound, and
of the ascension of a soul into the infinite on the wings
of that sentiment.'

'Whenever I go to an opera, I leave my sense and reason
at the door with my half-guinea, and deliver myself up
to my eyes and my ears.'
    LORD CHESTERFIELD; letter (23 January 1752)

'Nobody knows the Traubels I've seen.'
    New York's Metropolitan Opera director RUDOLF BING,
    following yet another dispute with his Wagnerian soprano
    Helen Traubel (1889–1972)

'Melba's voice stirs me to almost passionate admiration,
but admiration isn't joy; admiration doesn't satisfy; there
is no ecstasy in admiration.'
    SELWYN RIDER on Dame Nellie Melba, in *Triad* (1919);
    quoted in *The Guinness Dictionary of More Poisonous Quotes*
    (1992)

At a rehearsal for her first London appearance in
January 1723, as Teofane in Handel's opera *Ottone*, Italian
soprano Francesca Cuzzoni (1700–70) announced to the
composer that the air he had written specially for her
début did not suit her: 'It is too slow! I will have a fresh
air!' By this time Handel had had enough of her prima-
donna temperament. 'You are a veritable She-Devil,'
he shouted, 'but I would have you know that I am
Beelzebub, the chief Devil himself! You want fresh air,
I give you fresh air.' And so saying, he seized her by the
waist, dragged her to an open window and threatened to
heave her into the street unless she did as she was told.
Cuzzoni reconsidered her position and sang the song;
it made her reputation as one of the favourite sopranos
of the age.
[Incidentally, in John Mainwaring's *Memoirs of the Life of the
Late George Frederic Handel* (1760), there is a note that throwing people out of the window 'was formerly one of the
methods of executing criminals in some parts of Germany.']

Rehearsing his opera *Flavio* in 1723, the composer suddenly
found himself under threat from the leading tenor, a man
named Gordon. Taking exception to the way Handel was
accompanying him on the harpsichord, Gordon shrieked,
'If you can't follow me better than that, I shall jump on
your harpsichord and smash it to pieces.' 'Go right ahead,'
Handel replied, 'only do let me know when you will do
that and I will advertise it. For I am sure more people will
come to see you jump than to hear you sing.'

'Some of the singing parts in Handel's operas are
specially written for castrated men. These parts
get performed rather rarely these days, perhaps
understandably.'

A snippet in *What Hi-Fi?* (March 1998)

Following an opera performance at Covent Garden,
a music colleague visited the conductor, Sir Thomas
Beecham, in his dressing room. After complimenting
him on the orchestra's stirring playing, the visitor then
asked Beecham if he was aware of drowning the singers.
Beecham replied: 'I drowned them intentionally – in the
public interest.'

A would-be diva auditioned for a famous singing teacher
in Vienna. After hearing her audition pieces, the teacher
asked: 'Tell me, my dear, you are a virgin, yes?' The girl
admitted that she was. 'I thought so,' said the teacher.
'It tells in your voice. So sweet, but so innocent. Too
innocent. To be a great singer you must know life, you
must know suffering, you must know love. So go away
now. And experience! And when you have, come to me
again, and I will make you great!' Early the following
morning there was a tap on the teacher's door. It was
the young girl. 'I'm back,' she announced, 'and it's all
right now.'

When Maria Callas named her fee to sing at the
Metropolitan, the impresario Rudolf Bing was
astounded. 'Even the President of the United States
doesn't get paid that much!' he exclaimed. Callas
retorted: 'Then let him sing for you.'

A reporter interviewing Callas commented on the fact
that she was born in America, brought up in Greece,
and now lived in Italy. He then asked, 'What language
do you think in?' The canny diva replied: 'I count in
English.'

'I want you to sound like twenty-two women having
babies *without* chloroform.'

> Sir John Barbirolli, rehearsing the chorus of Vaughan
> Williams's *Sinfonia Antarctica*; quoted in Michael Kennedy,
> *Barbirolli, Conductor Laureate* (1971)

With her powerful voice, fine stage presence and
'commanding stature' (she was more than six feet tall),
contralto Dame Clara Butt (1873–1936) was one of the
most celebrated singers of the early twentieth century –
especially for her spirited rendering of 'Land of Hope
and Glory'. Legend has it that the singer was about to
leave for a tour of Australia when a chance encounter
with Dame Nellie Melba produced the following
response from the Australian star: 'So you're going to
Australia!' said Melba. 'Well, I made twenty thousand
pounds on my tour there, but of course *that* will never
be done again. Still, it's a wonderful country, and you'll
have a good time.' Melba then asked Dame Clara what
she was planning to sing, and offered the now legendary
advice: 'All I can say is – sing 'em muck! It's all they
can understand'. According to Ivor Newton in *At the*

Piano, a mutual friend asked Melba some years later if she had really given Dame Clara this advice. 'Of course not,' Melba retorted, but then added: 'in Clara's case, it wasn't necessary.'

'The most rococo and degraded of all forms of art.'
    WILLIAM MORRIS (1834–96) about opera; quoted in
    Chambers Music Quotations (1991)

'Of course I am nervous. Each time I sing I feel there is someone waiting to destroy me, and I must fight like a bull to hold my own. The artist who boasts he is never nervous is not an artist – he is a liar or a fool.'
    CARUSO; quoted by Dorothy Caruso, *Enrico Caruso: His Life and Death* (1945)

There is a terrible fear that lurks in the mind of almost every live performer, and that is the fear of 'drying', forgetting what comes next. In her *Life of Kathleen Ferrier*, Winifred Ferrier quotes a tale by the pianist and accompanist Margot Pacey: 'She [Kathleen] could get away with anything in those days, just as later she could twist the most sophisticated audience round her little finger. I remember her singing some Purcell duets with Helen Anderson and forgetting her words at a certain bar. With complete aplomb she broke off – and apologized. They started again and

the same thing happened. Kathleen started to laugh
– and soon the hall was in an uproar of amusement.
It was the most successful performance of the
evening.'

Still on the subject of 'drying': 'There's one small
comfort,' said Kathleen Ferrier, 'if I forget a word,
I *usually* find something fairly sensible to put in
its place.' Usually, but not always. During a recital
in which she was singing Handel's 'Where'er you
Walk', her mind went blank just as she began the
line 'all things flourish, where'er you turn your eyes'.
There was a split second of that dreadful panic
performers experience when their words go, but
then something came into her head, and she sang
that. Unfortunately, she might have got away with
'where'er they eat the grass' just once, but the line is
repeated: 'Where'er they eat the grass'. 'Was my face
red!' she admitted in the telling, and then added: 'It's
sometimes a bit awkward when the audience *can* hear
the words!'

Hoping for a sporting quote, a reporter once asked
Enrico Caruso what he thought of the baseball star
'Babe' Ruth (George Herman Ruth, 1895–1948). Polite
as ever, Caruso answered that he didn't know because
unfortunately he had never heard her sing.

On another occasion, this time after he had just sung
a duet with a soprano, who was perhaps better known

for her beauty than her voice, Caruso was asked how he liked her singing. 'I don't know,' he replied. 'I've never heard her.'

'I hate performers who debase great works of art: I long for their annihilation. If my criticisms were flaming thunderbolts, no prudent Life or Fire Insurance Company would entertain a proposal from any singer within my range, or from the lessee of any opera-house or concert-room within my circuit.'

GEORGE BERNARD SHAW (1894); quoted in *The Guinness Dictionary of More Poisonous Quotes* (1992)

When a singer insisted he knew better than Sullivan how a certain song should be interpreted, Sullivan told him: 'In future I'll get you to sing my songs first, then I'll compose them afterwards.'

Quoted in Hesketh Pearson, *Gilbert & Sullivan* (1935)

When a colleague referred to a certain tenor's lack of manly attributes, the conductor Hans von Bülow replied: 'My dear fellow, a tenor isn't a man: it's a disease!'

Blessed with a rare alto voice, the English countertenor Alfred Deller (1912–79) was able to sing many roles formerly associated only with castrati or women, particularly in the works of Purcell and Handel. Even though he wore a beard, the provenance of his naturally high voice was still occasionally in doubt. Before one recital in France he was asked: 'Monsieur Deller, you are – how do you say in English – eunuch?' Deller candidly replied: 'Yes, you could say I am. Unique.'

'The opera house is an institution differing from other lunatic asylums only in the fact that its inmates have avoided official certification.'

ERNEST NEWMAN; quoted in *Chambers Music Quotations* (1991)

When Milan's renowned opera house La Scala reopened in 1898 after a year's closure, Verdi visited the new management of Giulio Gatti-Casazza and Arturo Toscanini to offer his advice. The most important element of this was to pay no attention to the critics and a great deal to box-office receipts. 'Always remember,' he said, 'the theatre is intended to be full and not empty.'

In 1950, the distinguished director Peter Brook resigned as director of productions at the Royal Opera House, Covent Garden. He explained: 'After two years' slogging, I came to the conclusion that opera as an artistic form was dead.'

'[Sir Isaac Newton] said he never was at more than one Opera. The first Act he heard with pleasure; the second stretched his patience; at the third he ran away.'

REV. WILLIAM STUKELEY (1687–1765), Diary (April 1720); quoted in *Chambers Music Quotations* (1991)

An experienced and accomplished pianist was engaged to accompany a less experienced and even less accomplished tenor for a recital of Schubert *Lieder*. Things did not go well, and from the start it was clear that the tenor was far out of his musical depth. Nevertheless, the accompanist struggled manfully on, not only to accompany but to accompany in tune. Finally the interval arrived, and with it the last straw, as the tenor accused the pianist of playing badly. With exasperation the pianist replied: 'Young man, I have tried playing for you on the white notes, I have tried playing for you on the black notes, but I really cannot play in the cracks.'

If there was one thing W. S. Gilbert disliked, it was tenors. He found them temperamental and ready to walk out for even the slightest reason, and towards the end of his life he accused them of being the curse of every piece he had written: 'They never can act and they are more trouble than all the other members of the company put together.'

In *Don Juan* (1824), Byron also has a shot at tenors:

> The tenor's voice is spoilt by affectation,
> And for the bass, the beast can only bellow;
> In fact, he had no singing education,
> An ignorant, noteless, timeless, tuneless fellow.

'I loathe divas, they are the curse of true music and musicians.'

HECTOR BERLIOZ; quoted in *Chambers Music Quotations* (1991)

During the final rehearsal for a performance of *Messiah*, Sir Thomas Beecham stopped the proceedings, and said to the chorus: 'If you will make a point of singing "All we, like sheep, have gone astray" with a little more regret and a little less satisfaction, we shall no doubt meet the aesthetical as well as the theological requirements.'

'I know I have a reputation for bad tempers, but I am always having good tempers.'

    MARIA CALLAS; quoted in Dudley Moore, *Off-beat* (1986)

'An opera may be allowed to be extravagantly lavish in its decorations, as its only design is to gratify the senses and keep up an indolent attention in the audience.'

    JOSEPH ADDISON, *The Spectator* (6 March 1711)

Caruso and his wife accepted an invitation to join a French tenor in his box at a concert. They had scarcely sat down when Caruso told the Frenchman: 'Monsieur, Madame cannot remain unless you leave and brush your teeth.' The man departed immediately, and within a quarter hour returned with gleaming teeth. 'Good,' said Caruso, 'it is important to take care.' Later that evening, Caruso's wife remarked how strange it was that the poor tenor was not deeply offended. Caruso was surprised. 'On the contrary,' he said, 'the man should thank me. We remained. We might have left.'

'Opera is like a husband with a foreign title: expensive to support, hard to understand, and therefore a supreme social challenge.'

    CLEVELAND AMORY (1960); quoted in *The Guinness Dictionary of More Poisonous Quotes* (1992)

[Another source gives the 'wife' the foreign title; whichever, it's an interesting simile.]

When Sir John Barbirolli asked Kathleen Ferrier to learn Ernest Chausson's dramatic *Poème de l'Amour et de la Mer* for a concert the following year, the contralto expressed serious doubts about her French. Eventually, after much persuasion and encouragement she cabled her agent: ACCEPT CHAUSSON. TELL SIR JOHN TO PLAY LOUDLY TO COVER MY LANCASHIRE ACCENT.

    From Winifred Ferrier, *Life of Kathleen Ferrier* (1955)

'If an opera cannot be played by an organ-grinder, it is not going to achieve immortality.'

    SIR THOMAS BEECHAM; quoted in *The Guinness Dictionary of More Poisonous Quotes* (1992)

'I do not mind what language an opera is sung in so long as it is a language I do not understand.'

    SIR EDWARD APPLETON; quoted in the *Observer* (28 August 1955)

'Opera in English is, in the main, just about as sensible as baseball in Italian,' wrote the American critic and journalist H. L. Mencken (1880–1956). He also made this rather odd comparison: 'The opera is to music what a bawdy house is to a cathedral.'

'In the final analysis, opera is a poor substitute for baseball.'

> *Los Angeles Herald* (1986); quoted in *The Guinness Dictionary of More Poisonous Quotes* (1992)

'In opera, anything that is too stupid to be spoken is sung.'

> VOLTAIRE (1694–1778)

'Critics complained it wasn't opera, it wasn't a musical. You give them something delicious to eat and they complain because they have no name for it.'

> ROUBEN MAMOULIAN; quoted in *The New York Times* about his original production of George Gershwin's *Porgy and Bess* in October 1935

'Of all the noises known to man, opera is the most expensive.'

> MOLIÈRE (Jean-Baptiste Poquelin; 1622–73); French dramatist, who wrote in the new genre of *comédie-ballet*, for which Lully composed music

During a rehearsal of Ethel Smyth's grand opera *The Wreckers*, the leading tenor John Coates (1865–1941) stopped singing, and walked downstage to ask Sir Thomas Beecham: 'Is this the place where I'm supposed to be drowned by the waves or by the orchestra?'

'Going to the opera, like getting drunk, is a sin that carries its own punishment with it, and that a very severe one.'

> Writer, philanthropist, HANNAH MORE (1745–1833); letter (1775)

'I sometimes wonder which would be nicer – an opera without an interval, or an interval without an opera.'

> SIR ERNEST NEWMAN; quoted in Peter Heyworth, *Berlioz, Romantic and Classic* (1972)

'There was a time when I heard eleven operas in a fortnight ... which left me bankrupt and half idiotic for a month.'

> J. B. PRIESTLEY, *All About Ourselves* (1923)

'Bel Canto is to opera what pole-vaulting is to ballet: the glorification of a performer's prowess and not a creator's imagination.'

> NED ROREM, *The New Republic* (1972)

> Though opera is a noble craft
> Most operatic plots are daft!
> RON RUBIN, *How to be Tremendously Tuned in to Opera* (1989)

One of Dame Nellie Melba's greatest triumphs was as the doomed Desdemona in Verdi's *Otello*. If the applause for her death scene (in which Otello strangles her) reached a satisfactory peak she would revive, and signal for a piano to be brought to the centre of the stage. She would then proceed to accompany herself – and the audience – in an encore of 'Home, Sweet Home'. Having received more rapturous applause, she would then expire again on the bed, and the opera would continue.

George Bernard Shaw once described oratorios as 'unstaged operettas on scriptural themes, written in a style in which solemnity and triviality are blended in the right proportion for boring an atheist out of his senses.'

'Nothing can be more disgusting than an oratorio. How absurd, to see 500 people fiddling like madmen about Israelites in the Red Sea!'
>   REV. SYDNEY SMITH; quoted in Hesketh Pearson,
>   *The Smith of Smiths* (1934)

'Sleep is an excellent way of listening to opera.'
>   JAMES STEPHENS

'An unalterable and unquestioned law of the musical world required that the German text of French operas

sung by Swedish artists should be translated into Italian
for the clearer understanding of English-speaking
audiences.'

EDITH WHARTON, *The Age of Innocence* (1920)

'I sometimes think I'd like opera better without
the singing.'

JOHN AMIS; quoted in *The Guinness Dictionary of More Poisonous
Quotes* (1992)

'No good opera can be sensible – for people do not sing
when they are feeling sensible.'

W. H. AUDEN, *Time* (1961)

A very important critic, a man of lofty taste, visited
Verdi just as he was putting the finishing touches
to *Il Trovatore*. Eager for the critic's opinion, the
composer played him the 'Anvil' Chorus. 'What do
you think of it?' he asked afterwards. 'Dreadful,' the
very important critic replied. 'Right,' said Verdi,
'how about this then?' And he played the Miserere.
'What trash!' replied the very important critic, almost
wrinkling his nose at the smell of such base music.
'Just one more piece', said Verdi, and he proceeded
to play Manrico's rousing aria from Act III: 'Di
quella pira'. The very important critic shuddered.
'Unspeakable,' he managed to say at last. Verdi was
delighted. 'I can't tell you how glad I am to hear
you say all this,' he cried as he embraced the critic.

'What on earth?' spluttered the critic. And Verdi explained: 'I have been writing a popular opera, an opera not for purists such as you, but for the people. If you had liked this music, no one else would have. Your distaste assures me that in three months' time, throughout Italy, *Trovatore* will be whistled, sung, played!'

'Most sopranos sound like they live on seaweed.'
    SIR THOMAS BEECHAM, quoted in *Newsweek* (1956)

'If you can strike a low G or F like a death rattle and a high F like the shriek of a little dog when you step on its tail, the house will resound with acclamation.'
    HECTOR BERLIOZ (1862)

'She was a soprano of the kind often used for augmenting grief at a funeral.'
    GEORGE ADE, *Fables* (1899)

'Since he was a little on the lazy side, Mozart didn't start writing operas until he was twelve.'
    VICTOR BORGE, *My Favourite Intervals* (1974)

'You have taken too much trouble over your opera,' he [Handel] told Gluck, who wanted an opinion of *La Caduta dei Giganti*. 'Here in England, that is mere waste of time. What the English like is something they can beat time to, something that hits them straight on the drum of the ear.'

A. W. SCHMIDT, *C. W. Ritter von Gluck* (1854)

Critic's Choice

'What has music to do with a lustful man chasing a defenceless woman or the dying kicks of a murdered scoundrel? It seemed an odd form of amusement to place before a presumably refined and cultured audience, and should this opera prove popular it will scarcely indicate a healthy or creditable taste.'

From a London newspaper review of Puccini's *Tosca* (13 July 1900); quoted in Nicolas Slonimsky, *Lexicon of Musical Invective* (1965)

Hearing Jenny Lind sing 'Angels Ever Bright and Fair', the Bishop of Norwich is alleged to have remarked: 'What beautiful words! If only you would say them without the notes!'

> Yet I detest
>   Those scented rooms, where to a gaudy throng,
>   Heaves the proud harlot her distended breast
>   In intricacies of song.

SAMUEL TAYLOR COLERIDGE (1772–1834)

The actor and playwright Samuel Foote (1720–77) once asked a man why he was forever singing the same tune. 'Because it haunts me,' the man replied. 'No wonder,' said Foote, 'since you are forever murdering it.'

'A German singer! I should as soon expect to get pleasure from the neighing of my horse.'
    FREDERICK THE GREAT (1712–86)

'Opera is when a guy gets stabbed in the back and instead of bleeding he sings.'
    American broadcaster ED GARDNER (1901–63) in the 1940s
    radio show *Duffy's Tavern*

When Sir Thomas Beecham was rehearsing Quixote's death scene in Massenet's opera *Don Quichotte* with Russian bass Chaliapin in the title role, the diva playing Dulcinea twice missed the cue for her entry as the Don died with his devoted servant Sancho Panza lamenting by his bedside. After the second time, Beecham called the diva on-stage and said, 'Don Quixote has now died twice, and twice you have failed to come in. Why?'
    'It is not my fault, Sir Thomas,' said the tearful diva. 'It is him! He dies too soon.'
    'Madam,' replied Beecham, 'you are grievously in error. No opera singer ever dies too soon for me!'

'At Ranelagh I heard the famous Tenducci, a thing from Italy: it looks for all the world like a man, though they say it is not. The voice, to be sure, is neither man's nor woman's; but it is more melodious than either, and it warbled so divinely, that, while I listened, I really thought myself in paradise.'

TOBIAS SMOLLETT, *Humphrey Clinker* (1771)

[On the subject of 'the famous Tenducci' – the Italian castrato and composer Giusto Ferdinando Tenducci (1735–90) – Nicolas Slonimsky notes in his *Lectionary of Music* (1989), that the singer was a famous case of incomplete castration, and was in fact 'so manly' that he managed to elope with a mayor's daughter in England and produce a family.]

'The word, the flesh, and the devil lurk in the larynx of the soprano or alto.'

JAMES HUNEKER (1915)

Visiting Kathleen Ferrier's Hampstead flat to rehearse with her, the conductor Bruno Walter was introduced to her father. 'You must be very proud of your daughter,' said Walter. 'She's a wonderful singer and fast making an international reputation. Soon she will be world famous.' 'Yes,' her father agreed. And then with typical Blackburnian understatement, he added, 'Kath's not doing badly.'

From WINIFRED FERRIER, *Life of Kathleen Ferrier* (1955)

'Singers' husbands! Find me stones heavy enough to place around their necks and drown them all!'

ANDRE MERTENS, *Time* (1960)

It is recorded that Purcell, when composing one of his odes, could hear a chorister being rehearsed in one of his songs in another room. The singing master kept stopping the boy and trying to make him sing the ornaments exactly as Purcell had put them down on paper. Purcell called out, 'Leave the boy alone. He will ornament by nature better than you or I can tell him.'

> Quoted in M. and M. Hardwick, *Alfred Deller: A Singularity of Voice* (1980)

Sir Thomas Beecham was not renowned for his tact, particularly where singers were concerned. After a rehearsal of Wagner's *Die Walküre*, he remarked of the soprano playing Brünnhilde: 'Her singing reminds me of a cart sliding down a gravel path with the brake on, together with squeals of terror from the horse.' On another occasion, reminiscing about a production of *Carmen*, he said of the leading baritone: 'He made a mistake, thinking himself to be the bull instead of the toreador.'

Critic's Choice

'Signor Caruso sang so well that his appearance was easily forgiven, but when he was not actually singing, some of the audience were moved to observe that he looked like the Inspector of Police in the first act.'

> *The Times* reviewing *Madama Butterfly* in 1905

In his *Lives of the English Poets* (1779–81), Dr Johnson wrote of Italian opera: 'An exotic and irrational entertainment, which has always been combated, and always has prevailed.'

In a letter to a friend, the novelist William Makepeace Thackeray (1811–63) described a visit to the opera in 1850 to see 'the Swedish Nightingale', Jenny Lind: 'At the end of the first act we agreed to come away. It struck me as atrociously stupid. I was thinking of something else the whole time she was jugulating away, and O! I was so glad to get to the end and have a cigar.'

'How wonderful opera would be if there were no singers.'
  GIOACHINO ROSSINI

'I am convinced that people applaud a prima donna as they do the feats of the strong man at a fair. The sensations are painfully disagreeable, hard to endure, but one is so glad when it is all over that one cannot help rejoicing.'
  JEAN-JACQUES ROUSSEAU, *La Nouvelle Héloïse* (1761)

John Ruskin about Italian singers: 'Of bestial howling, and entirely frantic vomiting-up of damned souls through their still carnal throats, I have heard more than, please God, I will never endure the hearing of again, in one of His summers.'

'Tenors are usually short, stout men (except when they are Wagnerian tenors, in which case they are large, stout men) made up predominantly of lungs, rope-sized vocal cords, large frontal sinuses, thick necks, thick heads, tantrums, and amour propre. It is certain that they are a race apart, a race that tends to operate reflexively rather than with due process of thought.'

HAROLD C. SCHONBERG, *Show Magazine* (1961)

'Not sung by Caruso, Jenny Lind, John McCormack, Harry Lauder or the Village Nightingale.'

CHARLES IVES; inscription on one of his songs

The first musician to be knighted was the composer Henry Rowley Bishop (1786–1855) in 1842. Among other accomplishments, he was a founder-member of the Philharmonic Society, music director of Covent Garden, and of Drury Lane, where his most ambitious work, the opera *Aladdin*, was produced in 1826. Sir Henry is now almost completely forgotten except for 'Home, Sweet Home', which he included in his 1823 opera *Clari, or The Maid of Milan*.

'Baritones are the born villains in opera.'

LEONARD WARREN, *New York World-Telegram and Sun* (1957)

'Opera: it is a sham art. Large, plain, middle-aged women galumph around posing as pretty young girls

singing to portly, plain middle-aged men posing as
handsome young boys.'

WOODROW WYATT, *To the Point* (1981)

'If an opera doesn't cost a lot, frankly it just isn't
any good.'

HERMAN GEIGER-TOREL, Director of the Canadian Opera
Company; quoted in Canada's *Weekend Magazine* (15 December
1973)

'If music in general is an imitation of history, opera
in particular is an imitation of human wilfulness; it is
rooted in the fact that we not only have feelings but
insist upon having them at whatever cost to ourselves ...
The quality common to all the great operatic roles,
e.g. Don Giovanni, Norma, Lucia, Tristan, Isolde,
Brünnhilde, is that each of them is a passionate and
wilful state of being. In real life they would all be bores,
even Don Giovanni.'

W. H. AUDEN (1907–73), *The Dyer's Hand*, Part 8, *Notes on
Music and Opera* (1962)

'I never can hear a crowd of people singing and
gesticulating, all together, at an Italian opera, without
fancying myself at Athens, listening to that particular
tragedy, by Sophocles, in which he introduces a full
chorus of turkeys, who set about bewailing the death of
Meleager.'

EDGAR ALLAN POE (1809-45), 'Marginalia'; in *Southern
Literary Messenger* (July 1849)

'If I weren't reasonably placid, I don't think I could cope with this sort of life. To be a diva, you've got to be absolutely like a horse.'

> JOAN SUTHERLAND (born 1926); quoted by Winthrop Sargeant in *Divas: Impressions of Six Opera Superstars*, 'Joan Sutherland' (1959)

'A writer of operatic librettos, if he wishes to be modern, must not have read the Greek and Latin classic authors, nor should he do so in the future. After all, the old Greeks and Romans never read modern writers ... For the finale of his opera he should write a magnificent scene with more elaborate effects, so that the audience will not walk out before the work is half over. He should conclude with the customary chorus in praise of the sun, the moon, or the impresario.'

> BENEDETTO MARCELLO (1686–1739), *Il Teatro alla Moda* (1720); quoted in *Chambers Music Quotations* (1991)

In Mozart's opera *Don Giovanni*, there is a part in the finale in which the eponymous seducer seizes Zerlina. At this point, she is supposed to scream. Unfortunately, the singer in the original role was finding it difficult to emote with the right sort of scream. Again and again Mozart rehearsed the section, but all that emerged was an unconvincingly feeble noise. Finally, Mozart got the orchestra to repeat the piece, then went quietly on to the stage, approached the singer from behind – and at the right time he grasped her so suddenly and forcibly that she could not fail to shriek. 'That's the way,' said Mozart, 'do it just like that.'

'I am saddest when I sing. So are those that hear me; they are sadder even than I am.'
ARTEMUS WARD (1834–67)

Malcolm Sargent was conducting a Royal Choral Society rehearsal of Handel's *Messiah*. Dissatisfied with the way the ladies of the chorus were interpreting 'For Unto Us a Child is Born', he asked them to try again, with the advice: 'Just a little more reverence, please, and not so much astonishment.' Had they known Handel's habit of recycling songs (a fairly common practice then, as now) the singers might have been more than astonished. In its pre-*Messiah* days, 'For Unto Us a Child is Born' was a rather sensual love-song entitled 'No, I won't Trust You, Blind Love, Cruel Love'.

'My mother used to say that my elder sister had a beautiful contralto voice. This was arrived at not through her ability to reach the low notes – which she could not do – but because she could not reach the high ones.'
SAMUEL BUTLER, *Notebooks* (published 1912)

In December 1919, Caruso's wife Dorothy presented him with a daughter. Shortly after the birth, Caruso picked the baby girl up, carried her to the window, prised her mouth open and peered down her throat. 'See, Doro, she is exactly like me. Maybe she sing – maybe she don't, but her throat is the same as mine.'

'Wagner's music is better than it sounds.'

BILL NYE; quoted in Mark Twain, *Autobiography* (1924)

'This fault is common to all singers: when their friends ask them to sing, they are unwilling, but when they are unasked they will never leave off.'

HORACE (65–8 BC), *Satires*

'Gilbert could never see eye-to-eye with people who considered that their proper place was in the centre of the stage, and when a lady who was rehearsing the part of Josephine in *Pinafore* pointed out that she had always occupied that position in Italian Opera, he remarked: "Unfortunately this is not Italian Opera, but only a low burlesque of the worst possible kind." The lady continued her career in Italian Opera.'

HESKETH PEARSON, *Gilbert and Sullivan* (1935)

'In opera everything is based upon the not-true!'

PIOTR ILYICH TCHAIKOVSKY

How's this for a compliment? Meeting the diva Adelina Patti (1843–1919), Rossini told her: 'Madame, I have cried only twice in my life. Once when I dropped a wing of truffled chicken into Lake Como, and once when for the first time I heard you sing.'

'I'm continually breaking into song.' 'You wouldn't have to break in if you found the key!'

'When Harris is at a party, and is asked to sing, he replies: "Well, I can only sing a *comic* song, you know," and he says it in a tone that implies that his singing of *that*, however, is a thing that you ought to hear once, and then die ... Well, you don't look for much of a voice in a comic song. You don't expect correct phrasing or vocalization ... You don't bother about time. You don't mind a man being two bars in front of the accompaniment, and easing up in the middle of a line to argue it out with the pianist, and then starting the verse afresh. But you do expect words.

You don't expect a man to never remember more than the first three lines of the first verse and to keep on repeating these until it is time to begin the chorus. You don't expect a man to break off in the middle of a line, and snigger, and say, it's very funny, but he's blest if he can think of the rest of it, and then try and make it up for himself, and, afterwards, suddenly recollect it, when he has got to an entirely different part of the song. And break off without a word of warning to go back and let you have it then and there ...'

JEROME K. JEROME, *Three Men In A Boat* (1889)

'I am never happier than when I sing in my bathroom.'

ROBERTO ALAGNA; quoted in *Classic FM Magazine* (February 1997)

When asked why he doesn't sing in the bath, Luciano Pavarotti replied: 'Are you making a joke? Singing is work.'

During a visit to Germany, Caruso received an invitation to dine privately at Potsdam with Kaiser Wilhelm II. This happened every time Caruso went to Germany, and the tenor was not looking forward to another dinner with the Kaiser, who wished to talk only about music and the operas scheduled for the season. On this occasion, Caruso decided not to go. Martino, his faithful and ever-present servant (he even slept outside Caruso's door), pleaded with him: 'Signor, it is a royal command. You cannot refuse.' 'You are right, of course,' said Caruso. 'I will go, but on one condition, that you are invited too.' The Kaiser agreed, and Martino went too.

A stiff, formal, elaborate dinner for two, served in the banquet hall of the palace, was presided over by a major-domo who instructed an army of footmen in imperial livery by moving only his eyes. Throughout the meal, Martino stood silently behind Enrico's chair, totally unimpressed by his surroundings, and concerned only with his master and the food being served him.

As expected, the conversation took the form of a series of questions. What new operas would be sung this season? Which had this city liked? And what about that city?

Finally, when the singer had answered all the Kaiser's questions, the dinner came to an end. 'Herr Caruso,' the Kaiser said, 'you now will drink a toast with me.' Then for the first time he looked at Martino. 'To your servant, Martino. If I were not Emperor of Germany, I should like to be Martino.'

From Dorothy Caruso, *Enrico Caruso: His Life and Death* (1945)

After the interval at the Royal Opera House one evening, just as the conductor raised his baton to begin the second act, a lady in the audience leant over the front of the stalls, tapped him on the shoulder and asked: 'I wonder whether you might play the third act before the second act tonight? You see, my friend and I have a train to catch, and we do so want to know how it all ends.'

Critic's Choice

'Rigoletto is the weakest work of Verdi . . . It lacks melody . . . This opera has scarcely a chance of staying in the repertoire.'

Gazette Musicale de Paris (22 May 1853)

At a performance of Rossini's *Barber of Seville*, Wagner turned to his companion and whispered: 'How I love Rossini! But don't tell my Wagnerians; they would never forgive me!'

'It would be difficult to conceive of a more absurd art-form than that of opera. We are asked to accept that in moments of emotion it is natural for men and women to express their deepest feelings in trills and roulades. We are exposed to the spectacle of ladies in the rudest of health who tenaciously postpone their dying gasp in a cascade of endless portamenti. We see staid and sober gentlemen suddenly break into song when we

are convinced they would be more properly employed
in some respectable merchant bank or counting house.
Empires are destroyed in the space of an intermezzo.
Villains are overthrown in the time it takes to gargle an
aria. A five minute duet is all that is needed to pledge a
lifelong troth.'

JAMES HARDING, in the introduction to his biography
Massenet (1970)

'Tragic opera is just another disaster aria.'
JOHN H. CLARK

'A vile beastly rottenheaded foolbegotten brazenthroated
pernicious piggish screaming, tearing, roaring, perplexing,
splitmecrackle crashmecriggle insane ass of a woman is
practising howling below-stairs with a brute of a singing
master so horribly, that my head is nearly off.'

EDWARD LEAR; letter (24 January 1859)

In December 1950, Margaret Truman, daughter of
President Harry S Truman (1884–1972), gave a song
recital. Paul Hume, *The Washington Post* critic, wrote of it:
'Miss Truman is a unique American phenomenon with a
pleasant voice of little size and fair quality . . . yet Miss
Truman cannot sing very well. She is flat a good deal
of the time . . . she communicates almost nothing of the
music she presents . . . There are few moments during
her recital when one can relax and feel confident that she
will make her goal, which is the end of the song.'

The president was not amused, and immediately fired off a letter to the critic: 'Mr Hume,' he wrote, 'I have just read your lousy review of Margaret's concert. I've come to the conclusion that you are an eight-ulcer man on four-ulcer pay ... Some day I hope to meet you. When that happens, you'll need a new nose, a lot of beefsteak for black eyes, and perhaps a supporter below.'

Another tale about a president, this time Theodore Roosevelt (1858–1919). This may, of course, be apocryphal, but the story goes that after Roosevelt's death he went up to heaven. There, true to form, he barged hither and yon, directing this, ordering that, and generally making a nuisance of himself. Finally, St Peter decided that the only way to calm his ebullience would be to occupy him with a very responsible task.

Roosevelt was asked to set up a new heavenly choir. He fell to it with gusto, and after a few moments' planning, presented St Peter with his requirements. 'I need 10,000 sopranos,' he barked, 'and 10,000 contraltos, and 10,000 tenors. And hurry! The sooner I have them, the sooner we start!' 'Of course,' said St Peter, making a note of Roosevelt's demands. But then a thought occurred to him. 'Just a moment,' he said, 'you've forgotten the basses.' The former president raised himself to an imperious height and bellowed: 'I'll sing bass!'

Asked if she had any secret for singing Wagner's Isolde so brilliantly, Birgit Nilsson replied, 'Comfortable shoes.'

Asked what the ideal tempo for a particular song should be, the composer Fauré replied: 'If the singer is bad – very fast.'

According to the *Concise Oxford Dictionary of Opera*, the longest operatic encore of all time was of *Il Matrimonio Segreto* ('The Secret Marriage') by the Italian composer Domenico Cimarosa (1749–1801) at its première on 7 February 1792. The Austro-Hungarian Emperor Leopold II enjoyed the first performance so much, he invited the full cast and orchestra to supper, and then commanded them to perform the work in its entirety all over again.

'One can always count on Gilbert and Sullivan for a rousing finale, full of words and music, signifying nothing.'
    TOM LEHRER, US songwriter (born 1928)

'To Prince's Hall to hear a concert given by the Bach Choir at the eccentric hour of half past five. Unaccompanied part-singing was the staple of the entertainment; and I can frankly and unreservedly say that I would not desire to hear a more abominable noise than was offered to us under pretext of Bach's *Singet dem Herrn* and some motets by Brahms. I will not deny that there was a sort of broken thread of vocal tone running through the sound fabric; but for the most part it was a horrible tissue of puffing and blowing and wheezing and groaning and buzzing and hissing and gargling and shrieking and spluttering and grunting and generally making every sort of noise that is incidental to bad singing, severe exertion and mortal fear of losing one's place. It was really worse than the influenza.'

GEORGE BERNARD SHAW, *The World* (20 May 1891)

'People are wrong when they say that the opera is not what it used to be. It *is* what it used to be. That's what's wrong with it.'

NOËL COWARD, *Design for Living* (1933)

The accompanist Gerald Moore tells of a certain bass he once accompanied – or tried to. Finding Schubert's *Der Einsame* too high in the key of F and too low in the key of E, the singer then asked Moore if he had 'nothing in between'.

Following a visit to see Wagner's *Die Meistersinger* in June 1882, John Ruskin (1819–1900) wrote to Mrs Burne-Jones: 'Of all the *bête*, clumsy, blundering, boggling, baboon-blooded stuff I ever saw on a human stage, that thing last night beat – as far as the story and acting went; and of all the affected, sapless, soulless, beginningless, endless, topless, bottomless, topsiturviest, tuneless, scrannelpipiest – tongs-and-boniest – doggerel sounds I ever endured the deadliness of, that eternity for nothing was the deadliest – as far as its sounds went. I never was so relieved, so far as I can remember, in my life, by the stopping of any sound – not excepting railroad whistles – as I was by the cessation of the cobbler's bellowing.'

'Wagner has beautiful moments but awful quarters of an hour.'

ROSSINI; letter (April 1867), quoted in E. Naumann, *Italiensiche Tondichter* (1883)

In his biography of the French soprano Sophie Arnould (1740–1802), R. B. Douglas offers the following anecdotes about Jean-Philippe Rameau's latest opera *Les Paladins*:

'At one of the rehearsals . . . Rameau repeatedly told one of the actresses to take a certain air much faster. "But if I sing it so fast," the singer complained, "the public will not be able to hear what I'm singing about." "That doesn't matter," the composer replied, "I only want them to hear my music."'

Douglas continues: 'In spite of the reputation of Rameau, *Les Paladins* did not meet with any success, and was soon withdrawn – before the public had time to learn to appreciate the music, the composer declared; "The pear was not ripe," he said. "That did not prevent it from falling all the same," retorted Sophie Arnould.'

For the 1958 film version of Gershwin's American folk opera *Porgy and Bess*, the producer Samuel Goldwyn insisted that all the singers heard in the film had to be black. The original soprano hired to dub Bess was released after a test revealed that she did not sound the way the star Dorothy Dandridge looked. Goldwyn approached rising American soprano Leontyne Price, who had been a success with the role on the London stage. She was not interested in dubbing Bess's songs. 'No body,' she told Goldwyn, 'no voice.'

The title of Mozart's comic opera *Così fan tutte* (1790) means 'that's what all women do' – or thereabouts. The librettist, Lorenzo da Ponte, had used the phrase four years earlier in *The Marriage of Figaro*, in which Don Basilio sings: *'Così fan tutte le belle, non c'è alcuna novità'* – 'That's what all beautiful women do, there's nothing new in that'. Although the title, *Così fan tutte*, is rarely translated now – because it's not really translatable – there have been numerous attempts in the past. These range from the literal *Thus Do All* and *Thus Do All Women*, to the near literal *Thus Do They All*, *Thus All Women*, *All Women Do the Same*, and *They All Do It*, to more imaginative, if misguided, efforts such as *Women Are Like That*, *Women's Wiles and Loves*, *One Does Like the Next*, *Tit for Tat*, *What's Sauce for the Goose*, *The Two Aunts from Milan*, *The Girl from Flanders*, and even *The Transvestites*.

'*Parsifal* is the kind of opera that starts at six o'clock. After it has been going three hours, you look at your watch and it says 6.20.'

> Attributed to American conductor and writer DAVID RANDOLPH (born 1914); quoted in *The American Treasury* (1955)

Still on the subject of *Parsifal*, in *At the Shrine of Wagner* (1891), Mark Twain had this to say: 'The first act of the three occupied two hours, and I enjoyed that in spite of the singing.'

'If one hears bad music, it is one's duty to drown it by one's conversation.'

OSCAR WILDE, *The Picture of Dorian Gray* (1891)

All good friends
COMPOSERS ON COMPOSERS

Y ou'd think, wouldn't you, that those engaged in such a subtly brilliant activity as composing the world's most beautiful music would have a high regard for each other? Forget it! Follow us into this section and marvel at what, for example, Shostakovich had to say about Puccini: 'He wrote marvellous operas, but dreadful music!' Really! Clearly there's no such thing as a composers' union. The English composer Arnold Bax, unlike my first music teacher who adored J.S.B., once remarked: 'All Bach's last movements are like the running of a sewing machine'.

And I have a personal sadness – two of my all-time favourite composers are Berlioz and Mendelssohn, so why did Felix have to say this of Hector: 'He makes me sad, because he really is a cultured, agreeable man and yet composes so very badly!'

Beethoven on **Rossini**: Rossini would have been a great composer if his teacher had spanked him enough on the backside.

Berlioz on **Handel**: A tub of pork and beer.

Berlioz on **Saint-Saëns:** He knows everything, but lacks inexperience.

— on **Wagner:** Wagner is evidently mad.

— on **Wagner's** *Tristan und Isolde:* A sort of chromatic moan.

Bizet on **Wagner:** He is endowed with a temper so insolent that criticism cannot touch his heart — even admitting that he has a heart, which I doubt.

Brahms on **Bruckner's** symphonies: Greasy scraps from Wagner's table.

— on **Bruckner's** symphonies: Symphonic boa-constrictors.

Britten on **a passage in Sibelius's** Sixth Symphony: I think he must have been drunk when he wrote that.

— on **Brahms** and **Beethoven:** I have no great sympathy for either Brahms or Beethoven, although I admit that both are very great masters ... I have moved off them. They have failed me. Or I have failed them.

— on **Stravinsky's** *The Rake's Progress:* I like the opera very much. Except the music.

— on **Verdi:** When I hear a work I do not like I am convinced it is my own fault. Verdi is one of those composers.

Charles Ives on **Debussy:** Should have sold newspapers for a living.

— on **Mozart:** Effeminate.

— on **Tchaikovsky:** We know butter comes from cream, but must we watch the churning arm?

Chopin on **Berlioz:** He composes by splashing ink over his manuscript paper; the result is as chance wills it.

— on **Berlioz:** He makes too much noise.

— on **Liszt:** When I think of Liszt as a creative artist, he appears before my eyes rouged, on stilts, and blowing into Jericho trumpets.

Clara Schumann on **Liszt:** Most of all he gives me the impression of being a spoilt child. I am very near to detesting him as a composer.

Copland on **Rachmaninov:** The prospect of having to sit through one of his extended symphonies or piano concertos tends, quite frankly, to depress me. All those notes, and to what end?

— on **Vaughan Williams**'s Fifth Symphony: Listening to the Fifth Symphony of Ralph Vaughan Williams is like staring at a cow for forty-five minutes.

— on **Vaughan Williams:** His is the music of a gentleman-farmer, noble in inspiration, but dull.

Daniel Auber on **Wagner:** Wagner is Berlioz without the tune.

Debussy on **Grieg:** One has in one's mouth the bizarre and charming taste of a pink bonbon stuffed with snow.

— on **Richard Strauss**'s *Till Eulenspiegel:* An hour of original music in a lunatic asylum.

— on **Rimsky-Korsakov**'s *Scheherazade:* It reminds me more of a bazaar than the Orient.

Debussy on **Saint-Saëns:** Does no one care sufficiently for Saint-Saëns to tell him he has written music enough?

Delius on **Elgar**'s *The Dream of Gerontius:* Elgar might have been a great composer if he had thrown all that religious paraphernalia overboard. *Gerontius* is a nauseating work.

Dukas on **Brahms:** Too much beer and beard.

Elgar on **Stanford:** The stuff I hate and which I know is ruining any chance for good music in England is stuff like Stanford's which is neither fish, flesh, fowl, nor good red-herring.

Fauré on **Debussy**'s *Pelléas et Mélisande* (after attending the première): If that was music, I have never understood what music was.

Gounod on **Bizet**'s *Carmen:* Take the Spanish airs and mine out of the score, and there remains nothing to Bizet's credit but the sauce that masks the fish.
— on **Franck**'s Symphony in D minor: The affirmation of incompetence pushed to dogmatic lengths.
— on **Verdi**'s *Ernani:* It's organ grinder stuff.

Handel on **Gluck:** My cook understands more about counterpoint than he does.

Havergal Brian on **Tchaikovsky:** How shallow Tchaikovsky appears by the side of Franck! Almost an impostor!

Hindemith on **Richard Strauss**'s *Alpensinfonie:* Better to hang oneself than ever write music like that.

Holst on **Byrd**: Byrd's misfortune is that when he is not first-rate, he is so rarely second-rate.

— on **Stanford**: Stanford is all crotchets and fads and moods.

Hugo Wolf on **Brahms**: In a single cymbal crash from a work of Liszt there is expressed more spirit and feeling than in all Brahms's symphonies and his serenades besides.

— on **Brahms**: One single cymbal clash by Bruckner is worth all the four symphonies of Brahms with the serenades thrown in.

— on **Brahms**'s Second Piano Concerto: Anyone who can gulp down this Concerto with appetite can face a famine without concern. It may be taken for granted that his digestive system is enviable, and, in a famine, will function splendidly on the nutritive equivalent of window-panes, corks, stove-pipes and the like.

— on **Brahms**'s *The Peasant a Rogue:* There may be people who are serious enough to find this opera comic, just as there are people comical enough to take Brahms's symphonies seriously.

Mahler on **Schoenberg**: He is young and perhaps he is right. Maybe my ear is not sensitive enough.

Mendelssohn on **Berlioz**: A regular freak, without a vestige of talent.

— on **Berlioz**: His orchestration is such an incongruous mess and so slapdash that after handling one of his scores you want to wash your hands.

— on **Meyerbeer**'s operas: Melodies for whistling, harmony for the educated, instrumentation for the Germans, contra dances for the French, something for everybody, but there's no heart in it.

Prokofiev on **Stravinsky**: Bach on the wrong notes.

Puccini on **Stravinsky**'s *Le Sacre du Printemps:* The choreography is ridiculous, the music is sheer cacophony ... It might be the creation of a madman.

Ravel on **Berlioz**: Berlioz is France's greatest composer, alas. A musician of great genius and little talent.
— on **Saint-Saëns** (in 1916): I'm told that Saint-Saëns has informed a delighted public that since the war began he has composed music for the stage, melodies, an elegy and a piece for the trombone. If he'd been making shell-cases instead it might have been all the better for music.

Richard Strauss on **Schoenberg**: Only a psychiatrist can help poor Schoenberg now ... It would be better for him to be shovelling snow than scrawling on music paper.

Rimsky-Korsakov on **Debussy**'s music: Better not listen to it; you risk getting used to it, and then you would end by liking it.
— on **Scriabin**'s Fourth Symphony, *Poem of Ecstasy*: He's half out of his mind.

Rossini on **Berlioz**'s *Symphonie Fantastique:* What a good thing this isn't music.

— on **Wagner**: Wagner has beautiful moments but awful quarter hours.

— on **Wagner**: This is the man for whom the German people forgot Mozart.

— on **Wagner**'s *Lohengrin:* One cannot judge Wagner's opera after a first hearing, and I certainly have no intention of hearing it a second time.

Saint-Saëns on **Franck**: The word progress denotes something moving forward, and in moving forward you must leave something behind. Music is going forward and César Franck is being left behind.

— on **Richard Strauss**'s *Salome:* From time to time the cruellest discords are succeeded by exquisite suavities that caress the ear with delight. While listening to it all I thought of those lovely princesses in Sacher-Masoch who lavished on young men the most voluptuous kisses while drawing red-hot irons over their lovers' ribs.

Satie on **Debussy**'s 'From Dawn to Noon on the Sea' from *La Mer:* I liked the bit about quarter to eleven.

Schoenberg on **Kurt Weill**: What has he done? He has given us back the three-four bar!

— on **Richard Strauss**: He is no longer of the slightest artistic interest to me, and whatever I may once have learned from him, I am thankful to say I misunderstood.

Schumann on **Berlioz**: Berlioz does not try to be pleasing and elegant; what he hates he grasps fiercely by the hair; what he loves he almost crushes in his fervour.

— on **Donizetti**'s *La Favorita:* Marionette stage-music!

— on **Wagner:** For me Wagner is impossible ... he talks without ever stopping. One just can't talk all the time.

Shostakovich on **Puccini:** He wrote marvellous operas, but dreadful music.

Stravinsky on **Britten:** He's not a composer — he's a kleptomaniac.

— on **Handel**'s oratorio *Theodora:* It's beautiful and boring. Too many pieces finish too long after the end.

— on **Hindemith**'s music: As arid and indigestible as cardboard.

— on **Messiaen**'s *Turangalîla-symphonie:* Little more can be required to write such things than a plentiful supply of ink.

— on **Rachmaninov:** Rachmaninov's immortalising totality was his scowl. He was a six-and-a-half-foot-tall scowl.

— on **Ravel** (who was of Swiss-Basque descent): The most perfect of Swiss clockmakers.

— on **Scriabin:** A musical traveller without a passport.

— on **Stockhausen**'s works: More boring than the most boring of eighteenth-century music.

— on **Villa-Lobos:** Why is it, that whenever I hear a piece of music I don't like, it's always by Villa-Lobos?

— on **Vivaldi:** Vivaldi is greatly overrated — a dull fellow who could compose the same form over and so many times over.

Tchaikovsky on **Brahms**: He has no charm for me. I find him cold and obscure, full of pretensions, but without any real depth.

— on **Brahms**: I played over the music of that scoundrel Brahms. What a giftless bastard! It annoys me that this self-inflated mediocrity is hailed as a genius ... Brahms is chaotic and absolutely empty dried-up stuff.

— on **Handel**: Handel is only fourth-rate. He is not even interesting.

— on **Richard Strauss**'s *Der Rosenkavalier:* Such an astounding lack of talent was never before united to such pretentiousness.

— on **Wagner**: After the last notes of *Götterdämmerung* I felt as though I had been let out of prison.

Vaughan Williams on **Mahler**: A tolerable imitation of a composer.

— on **Stanford**: His very facility prevented him from knowing when he was genuinely inspired and when his work was routine stuff.

Wagner on **Brahms**'s *German Requiem:* Schumann's last thought.

— on **Meyerbeer**: A Jew banker to whom it occurred to compose operas ... A miserable music-maker.

— on **Offenbach**'s music: A dung heap on which all the swine of Europe wallowed.

— on **Rossini**: After Rossini dies, who will there be to promote his music?

— on **Schumann:** It is impossible to communicate with Schumann. The man is hopeless; he does not talk at all.

Walton on **Mahler**'s Third Symphony: It's all very well, but you can't call *that* a symphony.

Weber on **Beethoven**'s Seventh Symphony: The extravagances of Beethoven's genius have reached the *ne plus ultra* in the Seventh Symphony, and he is quite ripe for the madhouse.

Who's who

BIOGRAPHICAL BITS

Daniel-François-Esprit **Auber** (1782–1871); French composer
of orchestral works including violin and cello concertos,
and sacred vocal works. Today, Auber is best remembered
for his forty plus operas including *Fiorella*, *Fra Diavolo* and
Manon Lescaut.

Carl Philipp Emanuel or C. P. E. **Bach** (1714–88); German
composer and second son of Johann Sebastian Bach.
His *Essay on the True Art of Keyboard Playing* established
him as the leading keyboard teacher of the time. His
works include keyboard concertos and sonatas, symphonies,
chamber music, and also oratorios and church music.

Johann Sebastian **Bach** (1685–1750); prolific German composer,
and the best known of a distinguished musical family.
Mozart is said to have remarked about him, 'He is the
father and we are his children', while Beethoven described
him as 'the immortal god of harmony'. Renowned in his day
as an organist, he achieved his major standing as composer
only with the nineteenth-century revival of works such as *St
Matthew Passion*, *Christmas Oratorio*, the 'Goldberg' Variations,
and his six 'Brandenburg' Concertos.

Sir John **Barbirolli** (1899–1970); English cellist and conductor
of Italian and French parentage (his real name was Giovanni

Battista). He succeeded Toscanini as guest conductor of the New York Philharmonic-Symphony Orchestra in 1937, and in 1943 he returned to England as conductor of Manchester's Hallé Orchestra, where he remained until 1968. Barbirolli premièred works by Britten and Vaughan Williams.

Béla **Bartók** (1881–1945); Hungarian virtuoso pianist and composer, who developed a Hungarian national style. Works include the opera *Duke Bluebeard's Castle*, the ballet *The Miraculous Mandarin*, three piano concertos and six string quartets. In 1940, he settled in the US, and died there from leukaemia in poverty.

Sir Thomas **Beecham** (1879–1961); English conductor who is remembered as much for his barbed wit as his easy, elegant conducting. He founded the London Philharmonic and Royal Philharmonic orchestras. Among the many works he premièred are Richard Strauss's *Elektra* and *Salome*. He also championed the work of Delius and Sibelius.

Ludwig van **Beethoven** (1770–1827); German pianist, organist, viola-player, and probably the most famous and respected composer of all time, not least for the nine symphonies, the string quartets, the piano concertos and sonatas. Other important works include his only opera *Fidelio*, and his Mass — *Missa solemnis*.

(Louis-) Hector **Berlioz** (1803–69); French romantic composer, best known for his *Symphonie Fantastique*, *Grande Messe des Morts*, *Roméo et Juliette*, and *The Damnation of Faust*.

Ambrose (Gwinnett) **Bierce** (1842-?1914); US writer and journalist. As well as his best-known work, *The Devil's Dictionary*, Bierce published several volumes of sardonically humorous tales. He disappeared in Mexico, to a fate unknown.

Georges **Bizet**, originally Alexandre Césare Léopold Bizet

(1838–75); French composer, whose main claims to fame are the incidental music to *L'Arlésienne*, and the operas *The Pearl Fishers*, and *Carmen*, which he completed just before his death from heart disease.

Alexander (Porphiryevich) **Borodin** (1833–87); Russian composer and scientist. His best-known musical works are the unfinished opera *Prince Igor* (from which come the *Polovtzian Dances*), and the symphonic sketch *On the Steppes of Central Asia*. A member of the composers' group known as 'The Five' or 'The Mighty Handful', Borodin was never quite sure about his dual accomplishments. He once said: 'I am a composer in search of oblivion; and I'm always slightly ashamed to admit that I compose.'

Sir Adrian (Cedric) **Boult** (1889–1983); English conductor, principally of the City of Birmingham Symphony Orchestra, of the newly-formed BBC Symphony Orchestra, and then of the London Philharmonic. He championed Holst, Elgar and Vaughan Williams, and also wrote two handbooks on conducting.

Johannes **Brahms** (1833–97); prolific German composer of orchestral and chamber music, including four symphonies, also many songs and choral works including *A German Requiem* and the *Alto Rhapsody*.

Anton **Bruckner** (1824–96); Austrian composer, whose music during his lifetime was given a fairly mixed reception (though Wagner is supposed to have said: 'Bruckner! He is my man!'). Today, his fame rests mainly on his nine symphonies (the last unfinished).

Hans Guido von **Bülow** (1830–94); German conductor and pianist. Apart from his conducting skills, he is best known for his marriage to Liszt's daughter Cosima, who later deserted him for Wagner. From then on, von Bülow became an outspoken opponent of Wagner's music and a champion of Brahms.

Charles **Burney** (1726–1814); English musicologist (and the father of the novelist and diarist Fanny Burney). His *General History of Music* (1776–89) was long considered a standard work.

Ferruccio (Dante Michelangiolo Benvenuto) **Busoni** (1866–1924); Italian composer, virtuoso pianist, and influential piano-teacher and arranger. Apart from his piano compositions, his best-known works include the *Turandot Suite* and the opera *Doktor Faust*.

Samuel **Butler** (1835–1902); English writer, painter, and musi-cian, best known for his utopian satire *Erewhon*, and his autobiographical novel *The Way of All Flesh* (published posthumously in 1903). He was once described as having 'musical tunnel vision', probably since he adored Handel but loathed most other composers.

Sir (John Frederick) Neville **Cardus** (1889–1975); English music critic, mainly for the *Manchester Guardian*. One of the most highly-respected critics of the century. He was also a devotee of and writer on cricket.

Enrico **Caruso** (1873–1921); Italian tenor, nicknamed 'the Man with the Orchid-lined voice'. Combining singing with acting, Caruso was a regular at Covent Garden in London and the Metropolitan in New York, where he was noted for his performances in Verdi and Puccini. As well as being the most celebrated tenor of all time, he was – as one of the first people to recognise the importance of the gramophone – possibly also the most commercially successful singer.

Pablo **Casals** (1876–1973); Spanish conductor, composer, and – more importantly – one of the greatest cellists of the twentieth century. A devotee of Bach (he brought Bach's cello suites into the repertory), he once said: 'I need Bach at the beginning of the day almost more than I need food and water.'

Luigi (Carlo Zenobio Salvatore Maria) **Cherubini** (1760–1842); Italian composer of orchestral and chamber music, two requiems, other church music, and operas, including *Iphigenia in Aulis* and *The Water-Carrier*.

Frédéric (François) **Chopin** (1810-49); Polish composer and pianist. Described as the 'poet of the piano', he wrote almost solely for the piano: of his two hundred published works, one hundred and sixty-nine are for the keyboard. Noted also as the lover of George Sand, the pen-name of the author Aurore Dudevant. He is supposed to have said on his death-bed: 'Play Mozart in memory of me'.

Aaron **Copland** (1900–90); US composer, best known for his cowboy ballets such as *Billy the Kid* and *Rodeo*, and the orchestral *Fanfare for the Common Man*. 'The best we have,' said fellow American composer Leonard Bernstein.

(Achille-) Claude **Debussy** (1862–1918); French composer and critic. Once described as a great 'painter of dreams', Debussy is best known today for *Prélude à l'Après-midi d'un Faune*, *Clair de Lune*, and the opera *Pelléas et Mélisande*.

Gaetano **Donizetti** (1797–1848); Italian composer of more than sixty operas in Italian and French, including *Lucia di Lammermoor*, *L'Elisir d'Amore*, and the comic masterpiece *Don Pasquale*.

Sir Edward (William) **Elgar** (1857–1934); quintessential English composer, best known for his 'Enigma Variations', the oratorio *The Dream of Gerontius*, the concert-overture *Cockaigne*, and such 'popular' works as the five *Pomp and Circumstance* marches.

Mischa **Elman** (1891–1967); Russian-born US virtuoso violinist, especially noted for his sensuous tone. A child prodigy, he made his professional début in 1904.

Kathleen **Ferrier** (1912–53); English contralto, and one of the most loved singers of her generation in recital and oratorio. One of her greatest successes was in Mahler's *Das Lied von der Erde* ('The Song of the Earth') at the first Edinburgh Festival in 1947.

Sir W(illiam) S(chwenck) **Gilbert** (1836–1911); English dramatist and librettist. Together with Sir Arthur Sullivan, he wrote the most popular operettas of the past century, the so-called 'Savoy Operas', including *The Mikado*, *The Gondoliers*, and *The Pirates of Penzance*.

Charles (François) **Gounod** (1818–93); French composer and conductor (he was the first conductor of what is now the Royal Choral Society). His best-known works are the operas *Faust* and *Roméo et Juliette*.

Edvard (Hagerup) **Grieg** (1843–1907); Norwegian composer, described by Hans von Bülow as 'the Chopin of the North'. His main claims to fame are the Piano Concerto in A minor, the incidental music to *Peer Gynt*, and the *Holberg Suite*.

Mark **Hambourg** (1879–1960); Russian-born pianist and composer, who became a British subject in 1896, seven years after making his London début at the age of ten.

George Frederic **Handel** (1685–1759); German-born composer and organist (originally Georg Friederich Händel), he became a British subject in 1726. Haydn described him as 'the master of us all'. Among more than forty operas, twenty oratorios, cantatas, sacred music, orchestral, instrumental and vocal works, his *Messiah* (first performed in Fishamble Street in Dublin in 1742) stands supreme as one the most inspiring pieces of great music ever written.

Franz Joseph **Haydn** (1732–1809); prolific Austrian composer of more than a hundred symphonies (the total is disputed), around fifty concertos, eighty-four string quartets, twenty-four stage works, twelve Masses, and a multitude of other works. Among 'Papa Haydn's' innovations were the four-movement string quartet and the 'classical' symphony. Many of his symphonies have a 'samey' sound, but some are remarkable in their energy and sheer musicality.

Jascha **Heifetz** (1901–87); Lithuanian-born US virtuoso violinist of stunning ability; rightly considered one of the greats.

Paul **Hindemith** (1895–1963); German composer, violinist and conductor. His works include operas, concertos, and instrumental pieces. He left Germany in 1934, when his music was banned by the Nazis. Later he moved to the US, where, in 1941, he became a professor at Yale, and in 1953 at Zurich.

Edward **Holmes** (1799–1859); English music critic, best known for his *Life of Mozart* in 1845.

Vladimir **Horowitz** (1904–90); Ukrainian-born US pianist. Renowned for controlled yet forceful playing, and his interpretations of Liszt, Schumann and the late Romantics.

Dr Samuel **Johnson** (1709–84); lexicographer, critic and poet, whose position in London literary society won him the title of the 'Great Cham of Literature'. Apart from his criticism, he is best known for his *Dictionary of the English Language* and *Lives of the Poets*.

Michael **Kelly** (1762–1826); Irish tenor and composer. He created roles in *The Marriage of Figaro* in Vienna, and then worked in London as a singer, music publisher and theatre manager. He also composed more than sixty works for the stage.

Otto **Klemperer** (1885–1973); German conductor, regarded as the most authoritative interpreter of Austrian and German music, particularly Beethoven, Bruckner and Mahler.

Fritz **Kreisler** (1875–1962); Austrian-born virtuoso who became a US citizen in 1945. He also composed pastiche pieces which he sometimes ascribed to other composers, and, in 1919, had a Broadway success with his operetta, *Apple Blossoms*.

Charles **Lamb** (1775–1834); English essayist, poet and literary critic. He is chiefly remembered for his essays for the *London Magazine* (published in volume form as *Essays of Elia*), and for *Tales from Shakespeare*, which he wrote together with his sister, Mary Lamb (1764–1847), for children.

Oscar **Levant** (1906–72); US pianist, composer and writer, who championed the music of George Gershwin. His own works include film scores, some chamber music, and a piano concerto. He also wrote two witty books of memoirs.

Franz **Liszt** (1811–86); Hungarian composer, conductor, virtuoso pianist, and inventor of the modern piano recital. His works, some of the most difficult piano music ever written, include twenty *Hungarian Rhapsodies* and two piano concertos. He took minor orders in the Roman Catholic Church (and was referred to as 'Abbé'), but never became a priest.

Gustav **Mahler** (1860–1911); Austrian composer, whose works include ten symphonies (one unfinished), and the song cycle *Das Lied von der Erde* ('The Song of the Earth'). Mahler was also a conductor, principally of the Vienna Court Opera, and later of the Metropolitan Opera and the New York Philharmonic.

Dame Nellie **Melba** (1861–1931); Australian soprano, who triumphed in London, Chicago and at the New York

Met before the First World War. She possessed a perfect technique and pure tone, and inspired very thin crisp toast and the dessert, peach Melba.

(Jacob Ludwig) Felix **Mendelssohn** (-Bartholdy) (1809-47); German composer. From an early age, he was a first class composer (he wrote his overture to *A Midsummer Night's Dream* before he was eighteen), mainly classical in style, though his sources were often romantic literature and legend. Among his best-known works are the 'Italian' Symphony, *Fingal's Cave*, and the Violin Concerto in E minor.

Giacomo **Meyerbeer** (1791–1864); German composer, mainly of historically detailed operas on a lavish scale, among them *L'Africaine* and *Il Crociato in Egitto*. At one time he was highly successful, with a reputation to equal Rossini's. Another contemporary, Berlioz, described him as having 'the luck to be talented and the talent to be lucky'.

Pierre **Monteux** (1875–1964); French conductor. In 1911, he became conductor of Diaghilev's Ballets Russes, and premièred works by Debussy, Ravel, and Stravinsky's *Petrushka* and *The Rite of Spring*. Later he worked with numerous orchestras in Europe and the US.

Gerald **Moore** (1899–1987); English pianist, and one of the most celebrated and respected accompanists in the world.

Wolfgang Amadeus **Mozart** (1756–91); Austrian composer. He survived being a harpsichord prodigy at the age of four to become one of the most prolific and gifted composers of all time. Although he wrote most of his greatest works in the last five years of his life, including the operas *Don Giovanni* and *The Magic Flute*, and was at the height of his creative powers, Mozart died poor in Vienna of typhus, and was buried in an unmarked grave.

Modest Petrovich **Mussorgsky** (1839–81); Russian composer, and a member of the group of five nationalist composers known as 'The Mighty Handful'. 'An amateur with moments of genius', as Ernest Newman described him, Mussorgsky left us three great pieces: *Pictures at an Exhibition*, *Night on the Bare Mountain*, and the opera *Boris Godunov*.

Sir Ernest **Newman** (1868–1959); English critic. The most celebrated music critic of the early twentieth century, principally for the *Sunday Times*. He is also celebrated for his four-volume life of Wagner, studies of Beethoven, Elgar, and Liszt, and his books on opera.

Ignaz Jan **Paderewski** (1860–1941); Polish pianist and composer. As a pianist, he was famous for his interpretation of Chopin; as a composer, he wrote music in a late Romantic, nationalistic style. He was also a statesman, and, in 1919, became for ten months the first prime minister of the newly independent Poland.

Niccolò **Paganini** (1782–1840); Italian violinist. Schumann called him 'the turning point of virtuosity'. He was also a guitarist and violist, and composer. His works include six violin concertos, and many other violin pieces.

André **Previn**, originally Andreas Ludwig Priwin (born 1929); German-born American conductor, pianist, composer and arranger. Brought up in Los Angeles, he made his name initially in Hollywood (winning four Academy Awards for his film scores). During his time as principal conductor with the London Symphony Orchestra (1969–79), he did much to popularise classical music in the UK, and made a now legendary appearance with Morecambe and Wise.

Sergei **Prokofiev** (1891–1953); Russian composer. First as an *enfant terrible* pianist, then as a wildly innovative composer, Prokofiev approached all music – including opera, ballet and film scores – with intense energy. Among his best-known works are *Romeo and Juliet*, *Peter and the Wolf*, and his First Symphony, the 'Classical'.

Giacomo **Puccini** (1858–1924); Italian opera composer noted for his strong melody and dramatic plots in favourites such as *La Bohème*, *Tosca*, and *Madama Butterfly*. His last opera, *Turandot*, unfinished at his death, was completed by another composer, and premièred two years later.

Sergei (Vasilyevich) **Rachmaninov** (1873–1943); Russian pianist and composer. Among his best-known works are the *Rhapsody on a Theme of Paganini*, and the Second Piano Concerto, which played an unforgettable part in the film *Brief Encounter*.

(Joseph) Maurice **Ravel** (1875–1937); French composer, best known for *Boléro* (which was intended as a miniature ballet) and *La Valse*. Among his many other works are the ballet *Daphnis et Chloé*, and the fantasy opera *L'Enfant et les Sortilèges*. *He also orchestrated Mussorgsky's Pictures at an Exhibition.*

Nicolai Andreyevich **Rimsky-Korsakov** (1844–1908); Russian composer, whose music often incorporates Russian folk themes. He is best known for the *Capriccio espagnol*, the *Russian Easter Festival Overture* and *Scheherazade*. As well as his own music, he took charge of organising and 'improving' Mussorgsky's manuscripts after the composer's death.

Moriz **Rosenthal** (1862–1946); Ukrainian pianist, noted as a virtuoso technician, especially of Chopin, and for his wit.

Gioacchino (Antonio) **Rossini** (1792–1868); Italian composer, and one of the most successful composers in history. Altogether he wrote thirty-nine operas, including *The Barber of Seville*, *Le Comte Ory*, and *William Tell*. He retired from opera at the age of thirty-seven, and later concentrated mainly on sacred music.

Anton (Grigoryevich) **Rubinstein** (1829–1894); Russian pianist, composer and teacher. One of the greatest of nineteenth century pianists, but an altogether unremarkable composer. No relation to Arthur.

Arthur **Rubinstein** (1887–1982); Polish concert pianist, particularly celebrated for his performances of Chopin. He was sometimes confused with Anton Rubinstein: 'Often, when asked if I was his son and I answered in the negative, people refused to believe me.'

Camille **Saint-Saëns** (1835–1921); French composer and organist, best known for *The Carnival of the Animals* (which he wrote in a few days and suppressed during his lifetime), but equally deserving of attention for his concertos, sonatas, symphonies, and the opera *Samson et Delila*. Nicknamed 'the French Mendelssohn', and described as 'the only great composer who wasn't a genius', he once said 'I live in music as a fish in water.'

Sir (Harold) Malcolm (Watts) **Sargent** (1895–1967); debonair English conductor, celebrated for his outstanding choral conducting, and also for popularizing classical music at the Proms (where he revived the authentic tune of 'Rule, Britannia'), in children's concerts, and at the head of the BBC Symphony Orchestra.

Erik **Satie** (1866–1925); eccentric French composer, best remembered for his *Trois Gymnopédies*. Many of his pieces have odd titles; for instance, in response to a critic who claimed that his music had no shape, he titled his next work, *Three Pear-shaped Pieces*.

Artur **Schnabel** (1882–1951); Austrian-born US pianist and composer, who championed the challenging works of Beethoven and Schubert with great intensity and power.

Arnold **Schoenberg** (1874–1951); Austro-Hungarian composer, who rebelled against romanticism and invented the twelve-note method of composition now used in much of twentieth-century music. His best-known works are *Verklärte Nacht* and the choral *Gurrelieder*. During the rise of Nazism in the early 1930s, he left Europe and settled in the US.

Harold C. **Schonberg** (born 1915); US music critic, principally for the *New York Times*. He was the first music critic to be awarded a Pulitzer Prize.

Franz **Schubert** (1797–1828); prolific Austrian composer, who wrote more than six hundred songs, nine symphonies, fifteen string quartets, twenty-one piano sonatas — and all before his death at the age of thirty-one from syphilis.

Robert **Schumann** (1810–56); German romantic composer, particularly noted for his piano music and songs. He drew extensively on literature including Byron and Robert Burns. He died relatively young in a mental asylum.

George Bernard **Shaw** (1856–1950); Irish dramatist and writer. Before making his name as a playwright, he wrote under the pseudonym 'Corno di Bassetto', and was music critic for *The Star* and *The World* from 1888 to 1894. He also championed the music of Wagner and Verdi in Britain.

Nicolas **Slonimsky** (1894–1995); US composer, conductor, and writer on music; best known for his editing of music reference works, including *Thompson's International Cyclopedia of Music and Musicians*.

Dame Ethel **Smyth** (1858–1944); English composer and author. Her struggle to become a musician in spite of her father's opposition made her an ardent feminist. During the suffragette movement, her *March of the Woman* became a popular anthem. She composed a number of large-scale choral works, and enjoyed considerable success in Germany with her operas.

Johann **Strauss** II (1825–99); Austrian composer who became known as 'the Waltz King', composing countless famous waltzes including 'The Blue Danube'. Among his other works is the operetta *Die Fledermaus*.

Richard **Strauss** (1864–1949); German composer and conductor. Sometimes regarded as the last of the nineteenth-century romantic composers, Strauss wrote a number of symphonic poems: *Till Eulenspiegel*, *Also sprach Zarathustra*, and *Ein Heldenleben*. His fifteen operas include *Salome*, *Elektra* , *Der Rosenkavalier*, and *Ariadne auf Naxos*.

Igor **Stravinsky** (1882–1971); Russian-born composer, who became a US citizen in 1945. He revolutionised music with his use of primal rhythms and dissonance. His early ballet scores commissioned by Diaghilev include *The Firebird*, *Petrushka*, and *The Rite of Spring*. His later work includes a piano concerto, the oratorio *Oedipus Rex*, and the opera *The Rake's Progress* (with W. H. Auden).

Sir Arthur **Sullivan** (1842–1900); English composer, whose everlasting fame is assured with the 'Savoy Operas' he wrote in collaboration with W. S. Gilbert. Sullivan was also a successful 'serious' composer, and for his creation of *The Golden Legend*, he was dubbed 'the Mozart of England'.

Pyotr Ilyich **Tchaikovsky** (1840–93); Russian composer, remembered especially for his evergreen ballets *Swan Lake*, and *The Nutcracker*, and also for his symphonies, concertos, the '1812 Overture', and the operas *Eugene Onegin*, and *The Queen of Spades*. His music is characterised by great melodies and melancholy.

Jacques **Thibaud** (1880–1953); French violinist and gourmet. He formed a highly successful trio partnership with Pablo Casals and the French pianist Alfred Cortot.

Arturo **Toscanini** (1867–1957); Italian conductor who premièred

Puccini's *La Bohème* and *Turandot*. His performances at La Scala and at New York's Metropolitan Opera were noted for their intensity and precision. From 1937 until his death, he was conductor of the NBC Symphony Orchestra.

Ralph **Vaughan Williams** (1872–1958); English composer of strongly melodic music which reflected his interest in Tudor composers and folksong. *The Lark Ascending* has become a great favourite in concert and on record. He wrote nine symphonies, including the choral *A Sea Symphony*, and *Sinfonia Antarctica*; other works include the ballet *Job*, and the opera *The Pilgrim's Progress*.

Giuseppe **Verdi** (1813–1901); Italian operatic composer, noted for his memorable tunes, dramatic power and orchestration. He wrote a number of the works most frequently performed in the grand opera repertoire, including *Rigoletto, Il Trovatore, La Traviata,* and *Aida*.

Antonio (Lucio) **Vivaldi** (1678–1741); prolific Italian composer. Trained for the priesthood and ordained, Vivaldi wrote most of his prodigious output (more than four hundred concertos, including *The Four Seasons*) while music master at a girls' orphanage in Venice.

Richard **Wagner** (1813–83); German composer who developed an operatic style combining music, drama, verse, legend and spectacle. His massive *Ring* cycle remains a challenging favourite to this day.

Oscar **Wilde** (1854–1900); Irish writer and wit. As well as his epigrams and brilliant comedies such as *The Importance of Being Earnest*, Wilde also wrote a novel, *The Picture of Dorian Gray*, and *Salome*, the play on which Richard Strauss based his opera.

What's what
GLOSSARY

a capella without instrumental accompaniment (Italian, 'in the manner of the chapel', or choir).

adagio slow tempo; a composition or movement written to be played at this pace (Italian, 'at ease').

allegretto quick tempo; short lively piece, played not quite as fast as allegro.

allegro quick and lively; a movement or passage in this tempo (Italian, 'lively').

alto male form of female contralto voice, now usually applied to boys; also an abbreviation for contralto.

andante slow, steady; a movement or passage in this tempo (Italian, 'walking').

aria accompanied song for one voice, usually in an opera or oratorio (Italian, 'air').

baritone second lowest male voice, between tenor and

bass; also, an instrument with a range between tenor and bass (ultimately from Greek, 'deep-sounding').

baroque heavy, ornamented music of the 17th century and early 18th century.

bass lowest male singing voice; also the lowest note of a chord or the lowest vocal or instrumental part of a composition (from Italian, 'low').

bel canto term for a style of operatic singing requiring a beautiful sound and agile but smooth voice production; often used in connection with the works of composers such as Donizetti and Rossini (Italian, 'beautiful singing').

cadenza short, brilliant passage for solo instrument or voice near the end of a concerto movement or aria; although intended to sound improvised and spontaneous, cadenzas today are usually written by the composer (or sometimes by the performer), and well rehearsed.

canon piece in which a voice or instrument is imitated by one or several others starting later and overlapping in a regular pattern; similar to a round.

cantata choral work, especially on a religious theme, with or without soloists and generally with orchestral accompaniment (Italian, 'thing to be sung').

capriccio light piece in a free and lively style (Italian, 'sudden start or motion').

castrato (plural, **castrati**) male singer who has been castrated as a young boy in order to allow his natural high voice to develop in the soprano or contralto range.

chord combination of two or more notes played simultaneously.

coda final added section of a movement or piece, to bring it to a satisfying conclusion (Italian, 'tail').

coloratura florid or elaborate passage or singing style (Italian, 'colouring').

coloratura soprano female singer with a voice trained in such a style.

concert pitch (or international pitch) pitch to which orchestral instruments are tuned: 440 cycles per second for the A above middle C.

concerto composition for an orchestra and one or more solo instruments; usually in three movements (ultimately from Old Italian, *concertare*, 'to harmonise').

contralto lowest female singing voice.

counterpoint melodic material added above or below
an existing melody; technique of setting together two
simultaneous musical lines (from Latin, *punctus contra
punctum*, 'point against point', that is 'note against note').
See also **canon** and **fugue**.

counter-tenor adult male voice, higher than tenor; also
called male alto.

crescendo gradually becoming louder (Italian,
'increasing', from Latin 'to grow').

diminuendo gradually becoming softer (Italian,
'lessening').

diva great female singer; an operatic prima donna (Latin,
'goddess').

duet composition for two instruments or voices, or the
two performers presenting such a composition (from
Latin, 'two').

étude solo instrumental piece intended as an exercise
for improving technique; some composers such
as Chopin wrote études for public performance
(French, 'study').

falsetto artificially high voice; form of singing
in which a male reaches notes above the normal
male vocal range; sometimes used to imitate a

woman's voice or for comic effect (from Latin for 'false').

fantasia (or **fantasy**) imaginative instrumental composition in a free and unconventional form; also a piece based on a selection of popular melodies.

forte loud; a note, passage, or chord played forte (Italian, 'strong').

fortissimo very loud.

fugue vocal or instrumental composition in which a theme is introduced and developed as successive parts join in and repeat or imitate each other (ultimately from Latin for 'flight').

grand opera dramatic and emotional large-scale work, in which all the text is set to music.

intermezzo instrumental piece played between the acts or scenes of an opera or other dramatic work; an entr'acte; also short concert piece, usually for piano (ultimately from Latin, 'intermediate').

larghetto moderately slow tempo; slightly faster than largo.

largo slow and solemn (Italian, 'broad').

lento slow, slowly.

libretto text of an opera, oratorio or other dramatic musical work (Italian, literally 'little book').

lied (plural, **lieder**) term used to describe a German song for solo voice and piano (from German *Lied*, meaning 'song').

maestro term of respect for composer, conductor, or teacher of music (ultimately from Latin for 'master').
mezzo middle, or medium (from Italian, 'half'); also short for mezzo soprano.

mezzo forte 'quite loud'.

mezzo piano 'quite soft'.

mezzo soprano female voice midway between soprano and contralto.

nocturne short, lyrical – and occasionally melancholic – piece, usually for piano (from French, 'night piece').

opera drama generally sung throughout with orchestral accompaniment; the word is an abbreviation of the Italian phrase *opera in musica* – 'work in music'.

opera buffa comic opera (from Italian, *buffo*, 'comic').

opera seria serious opera (including grand opera).

operetta musical work for the stage, with songs interspersed with spoken dialogue; also called 'light opera'.

opus musical composition, used with a number to designate the order of a composer's works, though not necessarily the order of writing; the word is usually abbreviated as 'op.', for instance 'op.17' (from Latin, 'work').

oratorio religious musical composition for soloists, chorus and orchestra (from Late Latin, 'prayer hall').

overture orchestral music generally composed as the introduction to an opera, oratorio or play (ultimately from Latin for 'an opening').

perfect pitch the ability to identify the pitch of any note heard, or to sing any given note without the aid of an instrument or tuning-fork (also known as **absolute pitch**).

pianissimo very softly or quietly.

piano musical direction for softly, quietly (from Latin for 'smooth', 'even').

pitch relative highness or lowness of a note.

pizzicato played by plucking with the fingers on a stringed instrument such as a violin; also a passage or notes played in this manner (Italian, 'twitched').

polka piece of music for a lively dance originating in Bohemia; the dance, usually performed with a partner, has a pattern of three steps followed by a hop (from Czech *pulka*, 'half-step').

portamento (plural, **portamenti**) slide produced by a voice or instrument in passing from one note to another higher or lower without any break in the sound (Italian, literally 'a carrying').

prima donna first or principal female singer in an opera cast; even more important in the hierarchy (if such were needed) is **prima donna assoluta**, the 'absolutely principal'; for the chief male singer in an opera, the term is **primo uomo**.

primo tenore first or principal tenor in an opera.

recitative vocal passage delivered – or declaimed – in a speechlike manner; frequently used in operas, oratorios and cantatas.

rhapsody romantic, lyrical work usually in one movement, often with a melodic content based on folk tunes; for example, Liszt's Hungarian Rhapsodies (ultimately from Greek for 'sew songs together').

roulade melodic embellishment, especially in vocal music (from French, 'a rolling').

rubato performed at slightly faster or slower tempo than that marked to permit more expression (from Italian, *tempo rubato*, 'stolen time').

scherzo type of lively movement, usually in 3/4 time (ultimately from German for 'to joke', 'leap for joy').

serenade light music, originally played or sung by a lover to his sweetheart outdoors in the evening (ultimately from Latin for 'serene').

sforzando suddenly and strongly accented (from Latin for 'force').

sinfonietta symphony that is short in length, or one that uses a small orchestra.

sonata work in three or four movements for piano, violin, cello or other instrument (from Italian for 'sounded', as opposed to **cantata**, 'sung').

soprano highest female singing voice; also used for boy singers, who are often called trebles (ultimately from Latin for 'above').

sostenuto in a sustained or prolonged manner; a passage played or sung in this manner.

sotto voce very softly (Italian, 'under the voice').

suite light instrumental piece in several loosely connected movements; also composition based on a selection from a larger musical work, such as an opera or ballet (from Old French for 'following').

symphony large-scale orchestral work usually in four movements, although some shorter symphonies are in one movement.

tempo the 'speed' at which a piece of music is to be played or sung.

tenor highest common male singing voice (ultimately from Latin 'to hold').

toccata composition for keyboard, particularly the organ, intended to demonstrate the performer's virtuosity (ultimately from Latin, 'to touch').

virtuoso (plural, **virtuosos** or **virtuosi**) musician with brilliant ability or technique (from Latin for 'virtuous', 'skilful').

INDEX

INDEX

[315]

INDEX

INDEX

INDEX

Acknowledgements

The anecdotes, notes and quotes have been collected from a wide variety of sources: some alive, some not, some conflicting, some more reliable than others. In addition to the many friends and colleagues who have aided and abetted us, special thanks are due to Clive Burton, Richenda Carey, Harry Dickman, Béatrice Frei, Patrick Harris, Clare Howse, the late Archie Newman, Karolyn Shindler, Jon Thurley, Charlotte Barton and Rupert Lancaster at Hodder, and Robert O'Dowd and Rob Weinberg at Classic FM.

Thanks are due also to the following books and publications for both foreground and background information, particularly when considering several versions of the same anecdote or quote: *The Book of Musical Anecdotes* by Norman Lebrecht (1985); *Chambers Music Quotations* (1991); *The Elephant that Swallowed a Nightingale* (1981), and *Peacocks on the Podium* (1982), both by Charles Neilson Gattey; *The Guinness Dictionary of Poisonous Quotes* (1991), and *The Guinness Dictionary of More Poisonous Quotes* (1992); *Lexicon of Musical Invective* (1965) and *Lectionary of Music* (1989), both by Nicolas Slonimsky; *The New Grove Dictionary of Music and Musicians* (5th edition, 1954; 6th edition, 1980); *Opera Anecdotes* by Ethan Mordden (1985); *The Oxford Companion to Music* (10th edition, 1970); *Thesaurus of Anecdotes*, edited by Edmund Fuller (1942).

The authors would also like to acknowledge and thank for permission to quote material in copyright:

Chambers Harrap Publishers Ltd for extracts from *Ego 4* and *Ego 7* by James Agate; reproduced by permission. Robson Books Ltd for excerpts from *Beecham Stories: Anecdotes, Sayings and Impressions of Sir Thomas Beecham*, edited by Harold Atkins and Archie Newman, reproduced by permission. The verses by E C Bentley, reproduced with permission of Curtis Brown Ltd, London, on behalf of the Estate of E C Bentley; copyright the Estate of E C Bentley. Approximately 84 words (page 146) from *My Own Trumpet* by Sir Adrian Boult CH (Hamish Hamilton, 1973) copyright © Sir Adrian Boult, 1973;

ACKNOWLEDGEMENTS

reproduced by permission of Penguin Books Ltd. Woburn Press for extracts from *My Favourite Intervals* by Victor Borge, reproduced by permission. The extract from *Silence* by John Cage reproduced by permission of Marion Boyars Publishers, London and New York. The extract from *The Glory of the Hummingbird* (1974) by Peter de Vries, reprinted by permission of Abner Stein. Approximately 388 words slightly adapted from pages 43, 62, 84, 135 of *The Life of Kathleen Ferrier* by Winifred Ferrier (Hamish Hamilton, 1955) copyright Winifred Ferrier, 1955; reproduced by permission of Penguin Books Ltd. The extract from *Howards End* by E M Forster, by permission of The Provost and Scholars of King's College, Cambridge, and the Society of Authors as the literary representatives of the E M Forster Estate. The extract from *My Life* by Tito Gobbi with Ida Cook (Macdonald, 1979) by kind permission of Rupert Crew Limited. Thames Publishing for the extract from Cecil Gray's *Notebooks*, reproduced by permission. Michal Macphail and the Hambourg family for permission to quote from their father's book *The Eighth Octave*. The extract from *A Farewell to Arms* by Ernest Hemingway, reproduced by permission of Jonathan Cape Ltd. The extracts from *Gounod* (Allen & Unwin, 1973) and *Massenet* (Dent, 1970) © James Harding, are reproduced by permission of Peake Associates. Mrs Gerard Hoffnung for permission to quote from Gerard Hoffnung. *The Washington Post* for the extract from a review by Paul Hume, © 1950, *The Washington Post*, reprinted with permission. For the extract from the *Letters of D H Lawrence* Vol.1 edited by J T Boulton, reproduced by permission of Laurence Pollinger Ltd, the Estate of Frieda Lawrence Ravagli and Cambridge University Press. From *A Smattering of Ignorance* by Oscar Levant. Copyright 1939, 1940 by Oscar Levant; used by permission of Doubleday, a division of Bantam Doubleday Dell Publishing Group, Inc. Approximately 258 words (pp 28, 220, 246) from *Am I Too Loud?* by Gerald Moore (Hamish Hamilton, 1962) copyright © 1962 by Gerald Moore; reproduced by permission of Penguin Books Ltd. Robson Books Ltd for the excerpts from *Off-beat* by Dudley Moore, reproduced by permission. The extracts from *No Minor Chords* © 1991 by André Previn; extracted from *No Minor Chords* published by Doubleday, a division of Transworld Publishers Ltd; all rights reserved. From the anecdote by André Previn in Robert Morley's *Book of Bricks*, by permission of Weidenfeld and Nicolson. The extract from *All About Ourselves* by J B Priestley is reprinted by permission of the Peters Fraser & Dunlop Group Ltd on behalf of the Estate of J

B Priestley. For the couplet by Ron Rubin from *How to be Tremendously Tuned in to Opera*, edited by E O Parrott and published by Penguin Books, reproduced by permission of Campbell Thomson & McLaughlin Limited, © Ron Rubin 1989. Approximately 212 words from pp 293, 445, and 304 words adapted from pp 346, 347, 443, 444, of *Malcolm Sargent: A Biography* by Charles Reid (Hamish Hamilton, 1968) copyright © 1968 by Charles Reid; reproduced by permission of Penguin Books Ltd. The extracts from *My Young Years* by Arthur Rubinstein, reproduced by permission of Jonathan Cape Ltd. For excerpts from *The Great Pianists, The Great Conductors*, and *Show* Magazine reprinted by permission of Harold C Schonberg and the Barbara Hogenson Agency. The Society of Authors on behalf of the Bernard Shaw Estate for permission to quote from the works and from the music criticism of George Bernard Shaw. David Higham Associates for the extract from *Impressions That Remained* by Ethel Smyth, published by Da Capo; reprinted by permission. The extract from *World within World* by Stephen Spender is reprinted by permission of the Peters Fraser & Dunlop Group Ltd, © 1966. The editors and publishers wish to thank The Calder Educational Trust for permission to reprint lines taken from *Schoenberg, His Life, World and Work*, H H Stuckenschmidt (tr. Humphrey Searle) © 1977. The extract from *Under Milk Wood* by Dylan Thomas, published by J M Dent, reprinted by permission of David Higham Associates. The extract from *Design for Living* by Noel Coward © The Estate of Noel Coward. The extracts by Donald Francis Tovey from *Essays and Lectures on Music* (1927) and *Essays in Musical Analysis IV* (1937) by permission of Oxford University Press. The extract from *The Mating Season* by P G Wodehouse, reprinted by permission of A P Watt Ltd on behalf of the Trustees of the Wodehouse Estate, © 1939. The extract from *My Life of Music* by Sir Henry Wood, 1938, reprinted by kind permission of Victor Gollancz, © 1938. The extract by Woodrow Wyatt from *To the Point*, reproduced by permission of Weidenfeld and Nicolson. The extract from page 41 of *Twentieth Century Music* by Peter Yates, published 1968 by Allen & Unwin, reprinted by permission of Routledge.

Every effort has been made to contact copyright holders, but if any have been overlooked, the publishers will be pleased to make the necessary arrangements at the first opportunity.